Western Civilization
Primary Source
READER

◇

VOLUME
II

Western Civilization
Primary Source
READER

◇

VOLUME
II

Megan McLean
University of Pittsburgh

Boston   Burr Ridge, IL   Dubuque, IA   Madison, WI   New York   San Francisco   St. Louis
Bangkok   Bogotá   Caracas   Kuala Lumpur   Lisbon   London   Madrid   Mexico City
Milan   Montreal   New Delhi   Santiago   Seoul   Singapore   Sydney   Taipei   Toronto

WESTERN CIVILIZATION PRIMARY SOURCE READER, VOLUME II
Published by McGraw-Hill, a business unit of The McGraw-Hill Companies, Inc., 1221
Avenue of the Americas, New York, NY, 10020. Copyright © 2003 by The McGraw-Hill
Companies, Inc. All rights reserved. No part of this publication may be reproduced or
distributed in any form or by any means, or stored in a database or retrieval system,
without prior written consent of The McGraw-Hill Companies, Inc., including, but not
limited to, in any network or other electronic storage or transmission, or broadcast for
distance learning.

1 2 3 4 5 6 7 8 9 0 FGR/FGR 0 9 8 7 6 5 4 3 2

ISBN 0-07-283723-3

Vice president and editor-in-chief: *Thalia Dorwick*
Executive editor: *Lyn Uhl*
Sponsoring editor: *Monica Eckman*
Editorial coordinator: *Angela Kao*
Marketing manager: *Katherine Bates*
Project manager: *Marc Mattson/Susan Trentacosti*
Production supervisor: *Carol Bielski*
Permissions editor: *Marty Granahan*
Cover design: *Marc Mattson*
Compositor: *Todd Sanders*

Cover photo (detail): © *Tate Gallery, London / Art Resource, NY*

www.mhhe.com

CONTENTS

INTRODUCTION

The primary source documents compiled in this volume are intended to accompany and supplement the narrative treatment of themes that most Western civilization textbooks provide. These sources were chosen to give voice to individuals who observed first hand the birth and evolution of Western civilization. The observations recorded in these documents bring to life the social, cultural, economic, and political trends that have shaped the course of Western civilization by giving students insight into how diverse individuals participated in and reacted to these transformations. Some of the historical personalities included here will no doubt be familiar to students; others are less well known because they viewed these trends and transformations from the margins of Western civilization. Yet all contribute to our understanding of the role of human agency in shaping historical developments.

Instructors may wish to use these sources as supplemental readings to a textbook, or as tools for encouraging classroom discussions. The documents could provide the basis for writing or research assignments. Many of the documents overlap slightly in terms of time periods and themes, and instructors may wish to employ two or three documents at a time to stimulate discussions of the diversity of experiences of a particular event or trend. Each document is preceded by a brief introduction. That introduction outlines the life of the author against the background of the major historical trends that likely influenced his or her work. Then the themes addressed by the author in the excerpted work are summarized, and the specific passage is introduced. A few discussion questions at the end of each introduction encourage students to analyze the sources critically in light of broader historical changes. Lastly, the source listings provide additional biographical and critical cites for the individual author and his or her work.

Megan McLean
University of Pittsburgh

CHAPTER 13

Madame de Lafayette
The Princess of Clèves

John Locke
Second Treatise of Government

Madame de Lafayette, *The Princess of Clèves*

The Countess of Lafayette, born Marie Madeleine Pioche de La Vergne, grew up on the outskirts of Paris. As a teenager she waited upon the Queen for a number of years, learning firsthand about the intrigues of the royal court. She married rather late for a woman of her class. The Count of Lafayette, a provincial nobleman, was a man twice her twenty-one years, but nonetheless a desirable match for a woman from a modest family. Their relationship may have lacked passion, but the Countess assumed control of her husband's business interests in Paris with enthusiasm. She remained happily in the city, while the Count pursued his interests at his castle in Auvergne. In Paris, she remained abreast of the developments at the court, and enjoyed the company of several notable writers and intellectuals, who admired her for her wit and reason.

The primary concerns of the courtiers in the mid to late seventeenth century revolved around love. Madame de Lafayette understood, in keeping with her times, that love and marriage were hardly reconcilable, yet love often led to tragic outcomes. *The Princess of Clèves* was first published anonymously in 1678 in four parts because Madame de La Fayette feared the novel might reflect poorly upon her reputation by implying that she herself had indulged in amorous indiscretions. The tale of a love affair between a married woman, Madame de Clèves, and the Duke of Nemours at the court of Henry II, the novel reflects more accurately the social milieu surrounding Louis XIV than the historical moment it purports to depict.

The book immediately created an outcry among Parisians for its unflinching portrayal of the duplicity and frivolity of courtly society. In the passage below, the mother of the Princess, reproaches her married daughter's suitor, the Duke of Nemours, by regaling him with a tale of the royal family's disastrous romantic liaisons. The Duke shows little patience with these reproaches, while the daughter, Madame de Clèves does not sense the dangers that such an affair might involve for her.

THE PRINCESS OF CLÈVES

Madame de Lafayette

"If you judge by appearances in this place," replied Madame de
Chartres, "you will often be deceived; what appears on the surface is
almost never the truth". But to return to Madame de Valentinois—you
know that she is called 'Diana of Poitiers.' Her family is very illustrious;
it issues from the ancient Dukes of Aquitaine; her grandmother was an
illegitimate daughter of Louis XI, and, in short, there is nothing but
greatness in her ancestry. Saint-Valier, her father, was mixed up in the
affair of the Connétable de Bourbon, of which you have heard. He was
condemned to death and taken to the scaffold. His daughter, whose
beauty was wonderful and who had already attracted the late King, did
so well (I know not what means she employed) that she saved her
father's life. The pardon arrived when he was awaiting the death-blow;
but fear had so seized upon him that he had lost consciousness, and
died a few days later. His daughter appeared at Court as the King's
Mistress. The journey to Italy and the King's imprisonment interrupted
this love-affair. When he came back from Spain and the Queen Regent
went to meet him at Bayonne, she took with her all her maids-of-
honour, among whom was Mademoiselle de Pisseleu, who later
became Duchess of Étampes. The King fell in love with her. She was
inferior in birth, intelligence, and beauty to Madame de Valentinois, and
she had only one advantage over the latter—that of extreme youth. I
have heard her say several times that she was born the day Diana of
Poitiers was married. There was more hatred than truth in this
statement, for I am sorely mistaken if the Duchess of Valentinois did
not marry Monsieur de Brézé, Grand Seneschal of Normandy, at the
time when the King fell in love with Madame d'Étampes. Never was
there such hatred as that between these two women. The Duchess of
Valentinois could not forgive Madame d'Étampes for having deprived
her of the title of the King's Mistress. Madame d'Étampes cherished
violent jealousy against Madame de Valentinois because the King had
not severed his relations with her. This Prince was not scrupulously
faithful to his mistresses. There was always one who enjoyed the title
and the honours, but the ladies known as the 'little band' shared him in

turns. The loss of his son the Dauphin, who died at Tournon and who was believed to have been poisoned, caused him deep grief. He had neither the same tenderness for his second son, who now reigns, nor the same appreciation of his qualities: he considered that he was not bold or vivacious enough. He complained of this one day to Madame de Valentinois, and she told him that she would have him fall in love with her, to make him more lively and more agreeable. She succeeded, as you see. The love has lasted for more than twenty years, without being diminished by time or obstacle.

"The late King was at first opposed to it; and, either because he still loved Madame de Valentinois enough to be jealous or because he was urged on by the Duchess of Étampes, who was in despair at the Dauphin's attachment to her enemy, it is certain that this love affair caused him anger and chagrin, of which he gave daily evidence. His son feared neither his anger nor his hatred, and nothing could force him to lessen or hide his love: the King had to get used to it. This opposition to his wishes estranged him still more from the Dauphin, and attached him more to the Duke of Orleans, his third son. He was a comely, handsome Prince, full of ardour and ambition, with an irrepressible youth which needed moderating, but he would have become a very distinguished Prince if age had ripened his judgment.

"The Dauphin's rank as heir and the King's favour for the Duke of Orleans caused between the two Princes a sort of emulation that was pushed to hatred. This emulation began in childhood, and had always continued. When the Emperor passed through France, he gave his whole preference to the Duke of Orleans rather than to the Dauphin, who felt it so keenly that, when the Emperor was at Chantilly, he wished to force the Connétable to arrest him without waiting for the King's orders. The Connétable would not do so. The King blamed him afterwards for not having carried out his son's decision; and, when he banished the Connétable from Court, this reason had much to do with it.

"The estrangement of the two brothers gave the Duchess of Étampes the idea of enlisting the aid of the Duke of Orleans to support her in the King's favour and to thwart the Duchess of Valentinois. She succeeded in this. The Prince, though not in love with her, supported her interests almost as warmly as the Dauphin did those of Madame de Valentinois. That made two cliques at Court, as you may well imagine. And these intrigues did not stop at women's quarrels.

"The Emperor, who had retained his feeling of friendship for the Duke of Orleans, had offered several times to cede to him the Duchy of Milan. In the proposals of peace made later, he held out the hope of giving him the Seventeen Provinces, and of having him marry his daughter. The Dauphin was anxious neither for the peace nor for the marriage. He made use of the Connétable, whom he has always loved, to point out to the King the importance of not making his successor's brother as powerful as a Duke of Orleans would be if he had the support of the Emperor and of the Seventeen Provinces. The Connétable was all the more of the Dauphin's opinion because he thus opposed the desires of Madame d'Étampes, who was his bitter enemy and who ardently desired the advancement of the Duke of Orleans.

"The Dauphin, at the time, was commanding the King's forces in Champagne, and had reduced those of the Emperor to such an extremity that they would have entirely perished if the Duchess of Étampes, fearing that too great a success would make us refuse peace and the alliance of the Emperor with the Duke of Orleans, had not secretly told the enemy to surprise Épernay and Châtaeau Thierry, which were full of victuals. They did this, and, in this way, saved all their army.

"The Duchess did not long enjoy the success of her treachery. Shortly afterwards, the Duke of Orleans died at Farmoutiers, of some kind of contagious disease. He loved one of the most beautiful women at Court, and was loved by her. I shall not name her, because she had since lived so virtuously, and because she hid with such care her love for the Prince, that her reputation deserves to be respected. Fate willed that she should hear of her husband's death on the very day she learned of the death of the Duke of Orleans, so that she was able to hide the real cause of her affliction without having to restrain her grief.

"The King did not long survive his son: he died two years later. He recommended the Dauphin to make use of Cardinal de Tournon and Admiral d'Annebault, and he did not mention the Connétable, who was at that time exiled at Chantilly. Yet the first thing the new King did was to recall him and give him charge of affairs.

"Madame d'Étampes was sent away, and received all the ill-treatment that she could expect from an all-powerful enemy. The Duchess of Valentinois avenged herself to the full on her rival and on all those who had thwarted her. Her power over the King's mind appeared to be even more absolute than it had appeared to be while he was still Dauphin. During the twelve years the King has reigned, she has been absolute mistress over all. She disposes of offices and of affairs of State; she has had dismissed Cardinal de Tournon, Chancellor Olivier and Villeroy.

"Those who wished to enlighten the King as to her conduct have perished in the attempt. Count de Taix, Grand Master of Artillery, who did not like her, could not refrain from speaking of her love-affairs, especially that with Count de Brissac, of whom the King had already been very jealous. Nevertheless, she played her cards so well that Count de Taix was disgraced: his command was taken from him and— which is almost unbelievable—she had it given to Count de Brissac. Later, she made him Marshal of France.

"The King's jealousy increased, however, to such a degree that he could not suffer the Marshal's remaining at Court. But jealousy, harsh and violent in all others, was gentle and moderate in him, because of the extreme respect that he had for his Mistress; so that he did not dare send his rival away, except on the pretext of giving him the Governorship of Piedmont. Brissac passed many years there; he came back last winter, ostensibly to ask for troops and for other things necessary for the army he commanded. The wish to see Madame de Valentinois and the fear of being forgotten by her had perhaps more to do with his journey.

"The King received him very coldly. The Guises, who did not like him, but did not dare show their feelings because of Madame de Valentinois, used the Vidame, who was his avowed enemy, to prevent his obtaining any of the things he came to seek. It was not hard to thwart him: the King hated him, and his presence caused him uneasiness, so that he was forced to go back without any fruit of his journey except perhaps the strengthening in Madame de Valentinois of feelings that absence was beginning to weaken. The King had had many other grounds for jealousy, but he did not know of them or he did not dare to complain.

"I do not know, daughter," added Madame de Chartres, "whether you do not think that I have told you of more things than you wished to hear."

"I am very far, Madame, from thus complaining," replied Madame de Clèves, "and, were it not that I fear to be importunate, I should ask you further of many circumstances of which I am ignorant."

Monsieur de Nemours' love for Madame de Clèves was from the first so violent that it deprived him of the taste for, even of the memory of, all the ladies he had loved and with whom he had kept up correspondence during his absence. He did not even take the trouble to seek excuses for breaking with them: he had no patience to listen to their complaints or reply to their reproaches. The Dauphiness, for whom he had had a somewhat strong passion, could not occupy his heart in competition with Madame de Clèves. Even his impatience to go to England began to abate, and he did not urge with as much ardour as before the arrangements necessary for his departure. He often went to the Dauphiness' because Madame de Clèves was often there, and he was not averse to having people imagine what had been believed concerning his feelings for the Queen in question. Madame de Clèves seemed to him so precious that he decided to refrain from giving her any indication of his love rather than risk having the public know of it. He did not speak of it even to the Vidame de Chartres, who was his close friend and from whom he hid nothing. He ordered his life so wisely, and was so careful, that no one save the Chevalier de Guise suspected him of being in love with Madame de Clèves; and she herself would have found it difficult to perceive if the inclination she had for him had not caused her closely to observe his actions, which left no doubt in her mind.

She did not feel as ready to tell her mother what she thought of the feelings of this Prince as she had been to speak to her concerning her other suitors; without any deliberate intention of hiding the matter from her, she did not speak about it. But Madame de Chartres saw it only too clearly, as well as the inclination that her daughter had for him. This knowledge caused her real pain: she saw clearly the peril of this young girl, loved by a man as attractive as Monsieur de Nemours and feeling some inclination for him. Her suspicions of this inclination were completely confirmed by something that happened a few days later.

Marshal de Saint-André, who sought every occasion to show his magnificence, earnestly begged the King, on the pretext of showing him his house, the building of which was just finished, to do him the honour of supping there with the Queens. The Marshal was also very pleased to display before Madame de Clèves a lavish expenditure that did not fall short of profusion.

Some days before the date chosen for the supper, the Dauphin, whose health was rather bad, had fallen ill and had received no visitors. The Queen, his wife, had spent the whole day with him.

Madame de Clèves did not appear to be listening to what the Prince of Condé was saying, but she was paying careful attention to every word. She easily guessed the share she had in the cause upheld by Monsieur de Nemours, and especially in what he said of the suffering caused by not being at a ball attended by the loved one, for he was not to be at Marshal de Saint-André's ball, as the King had charged him to go and meet the Duke of Ferrara.

The Dauphiness laughed with the Prince of Condé, and did not agree with the opinion of Monsieur de Nemours.

"There is only one occasion," said the Prince, "on which Monsieur de Nemours agrees that the lady he loves may go to a ball: it is when he gives it himself. He admits that last year, when he gave one for Your Majesty, he considered that his lady-love conferred a favour on him by coming, although she seemed to be merely attending you. He thinks it is always conferring a favour on a lover to take part in a pleasure offered by him—that it is always pleasant for a lover to have his lady see him master of a place in which all the Court assembles, and successfully doing the honours."

"Monsieur de Nemours was right," said the Dauphiness, with a smile, "to approve of his lady-love's going to the ball; there were at that time so many ladies to whom he gave the title that, had they not been present, there would have been few people there."

Discussion Questions

1. What morals can be drawn from Madame de Chartres' story about Madame de Valentinois?

2. Why did a love affair hold so much risk for Madame de Clèves? Did men and women face unequal hazards when engaging in extramarital relations?

Sources

Madame de La Fayette, *The Princess of Clèves*, trans H. Ashton, London: The Nonesuch Press, 1943.

Stirling Haig, *Madame de Lafayette*, New York: Twayne Publishers, 1970.

John Locke, Second Treatise of Government

John Locke was born in 1632 to a family of modest means in Somerset. His father had fought in the Parliamentary army during the English civil war of the 1640s, and his family leaned toward Puritanism. He was educated at some of the finest English schools, and became a graduate fellow and teacher at Christ Church, Oxford in his 20s and early 30s, where he taught philosophy and studied medicine. He maintained an uneasy relationship with the Oxford colleges, whose deans disapproved of some of his early writings. Locke remained at the institution until 1665, and after a brief stint as a diplomat, joined the household of Anthony Ashley Cooper, the Earl of Shaftesbury.

Upon becoming the physician of the Earl of Shaftesbury, Locke entered into a world of political intrigue. His presence in the Shaftesbury household owed as much to their shared political leanings as it did to Locke's medical knowledge. The Earl, once a supporter of Charles II, had opposed Charles' increasingly absolutist measures and the imminent succession of the Catholic James II. Charles II reacted by dissolving Parliament, and Earl and his following were persecuted. Locke likely drafted the *Second Treatise of Government* sometime between 1679 and 1683 with the encouragement of the Earl of Shaftesbury, just as these events were taking shape. However, circumstances forced Locke to flee to Holland in 1683, where he remained until 1689 when the victory of William and Mary over James and the passing of a Bill of Rights in 1689 guaranteed his safe return.

His *Second Treatise* was not published until 1690, serving to explain the Glorious Revolution after the fact rather than to justify it, as the piece had been intended. Locke did not acknowledge authorship, fearing repercussions if the political climate again shifted. The publication immediately became an enduring classic in political theory. Locke's notions of limited government and the right to rebel inspired revolutionaries over the course of the next century, and his work remains popular because of his ideas regarding the inseparability of property rights, individual liberties, and a liberal constitutional state. In the sections below, Locke explains the advantages of government for individuals. Then he defines his conception of a commonwealth before exploring the limits of the legislative powers of within a commonwealth.

SECOND TREATISE OF GOVERNMENT

John Locke

CHAP. IX.

OF THE ENDS OF POLITICAL SOCIETY AND GOVERNMENT.

§. 123. IF man in the state of nature be so free, as has been said; if he be absolute lord of his own person and possessions, equal to the greatest, and subject to no body, why will he part with his freedom? why will he give up this empire, and subject himself to the dominion and controul of any other power? To which it is obvious to answer, that though in the state of nature he hath such a right, yet the enjoyment of it is very uncertain, and constantly exposed to the invasion of others: for all being kings as as he, every man his equal, and the greater part no strict observers of equity and justice, the enjoyment of the property he has in this state is very unsafe, very unsecure. This makes him willing to quit a condition, which, however free, is full of fears and continual dangers: and it is not without reason, that he seeks out, and is willing to join in society with others, who are already united, or have a mind to unite, for the mutual *preservation* of their lives, liberties and estates, which I call by the general name, *property.*

§.124. The great and *chief end,* therefore, of men's uniting into common-wealths, and putting themselves under government, *is the preservation of their property.* To which in the state of nature there are many things wanting.

First, There wants an *established,* settled, known *law,* received and allowed by common consent to be the standard of right and wrong, and the common measure to decide all controversies between them: for though the law of nature be plain and intelligible to all rational creatures; yet men being biassed by their interest, as well as ignorant for want of study of it, are not apt to allow of it as a law binding to them in the application of it to their particular cases.

§. 125. *Secondly,* In the state of nature there wants *a known and indifferent judge,* with authority to determine all differences according to the established law: for every one in that state being both judge and executioner of the law of nature, men being partial to themselves, passion and revenge is very apt to carry them too far, and with too much heat, in their own cases; as well as negligence, and unconcernedness, to make them too remiss in other men's.

§. 126. *Thirdly,* In the state of nature there often wants *power* to back and support the sentence when right, and to *give* it due *execution.* They who by any injustice offended, will seldom fail, where they are able, by force to make good their injustice; such resistance many times makes the punishment dangerous, and frequently destructive, to those who attempt it.

§. 127. Thus mankind, notwithstanding all the privileges of the state of nature, being but in an ill condition, while they remain in it, are quickly driven into society. Hence it comes to pass, that we seldom find any number of men live any time together in this state. The inconveniencies that they are therein exposed to, by the irregular and uncertain exercise of the power every man has of punishing the transgressions of others, make them take sanctuary under the established laws of government, and therein seek *the preservation of their property.* It is this makes them so willingly give up every one his single power of punishing, to be exercised by such alone, as shall be appointed to it amongst them; and by such rules as the community, or those authorized by them to that purpose, shall agree on. And in this we have the original *right and rise of both the legislative and executive power,* as well as of the governments and societies themselves.

§. 128. For in the state of nature, to omit the liberty he has of innocent delights, a man has two powers.

The first is to do whatsoever he thinks fit for the preservation of himself, and others within the permission of the *law of nature:* by which law, common to them all, he and all the rest of *mankind are one community,* make up one society, distinct from all other creatures. And were it not for the corruption and vitiousness of degenerate men, there would be no need of any other; no necessity that men should separate from this great and natural community, and by positive agreements combine into smaller and divided associations.

The other power a man has in the state of nature, is the *power to punish the crimes* committed against that law. Both these he gives up, when he joins in a private, if I may call it so, or particular politic society, and incorporates into any common-wealth, separate from the rest of mankind.

§. 129. The first *power*, viz. *of doing whatsoever he thought for the preservation of himself*, and the rest of mankind, *he gives up* to be regulated by laws made by the society, so far forth as the preservation of himself, and the rest of that society shall require; which laws of the society in many things confine the liberty he had by the law of nature.

§. 130. *Secondly, The power of punishing he wholly gives up*, and engages his natural force, (which he might before employ in the execution of the law of nature, by his own single authority,as he thought fit) to assist the executive power of the society, as the law thereof shall require: for being now in a new state, wherein he is to enjoy many conveniencies, from the labour, assistance, and society of others in the same community, as well as protection from its whole strength; he is to part also with as much of his natural liberty, in providing for himself, as the good, prosperity, and safety of the society shall require; which is not only necessary, but just, since the other members of the society do the like.

§ 131. But though men, when they enter into society, give up the equality, liberty, and executive power they had in the state of nature, into the hands of the society to be so far disposed of by the legislative as the good of the society shall require; yet it being only with an intention in every one the better to preserve himself, his liberty and property; (for no rational creature can be supposed to change his condition with an intention to be worse) the power of the society, or *legislative* constituted by them, can *never be supposed to extend farther, than the common good*; but is obliged to secure every one's property, by providing against those three defects above mentioned, that made the state of nature so unsafe and uneasy. And so whoever has the legislative or supreme power of any common-wealth, is bound to govern by established *standing laws*, promulgated and known to the people, and not by extemporary decrees; by *indifferent* upright *judges*, who are to decide controversies by those laws; and to employ the force of the community at home, *only in the execution of such laws*, or abroad to prevent or redress foreign injuries, and secure the community from inroads and invasion. And all this to be directed to no other *end*, but the *peace, safety*, and *public good* of the people.

CHAP. X.

OF THE FORMS OF A COMMON-WEALTH.

§. 132. THE majority having, as has been shewed, upon men's first uniting into society, the whole power of the community naturally in them, may employ all that power in making laws for the community from time to time, and executing those laws by officers of their own appointing; and then the *form* of the government is a perfect *democracy*: or else may put the power of making laws into the hands of a few select men, and their heirs or successors; and then it is an *oligarchy*: or else into the hands of one man, and then it is a *monarchy*: if to him and his heirs, it is an *hereditary monarchy*: if to him only for life, but upon his death the power only of nominating a successor to return to them; an *elective monarchy*. And so accordingly of these the community may make compounded and mixed forms of government, as they think good. And if the legislative power be at first given by the majority to one or more persons only for their lives, or any limited time, and then the supreme power to revert to them again; when it is so reverted, the community may dispose of it again anew into what hands they please, and so constitute a new form of government: for the *form of government depending upon the placing the* supreme power, which is the legislative, it being impossible to conceive that an inferior power should prescribe to a superior, or any but the supreme make laws, according as the power of making laws is placed, such is the *form of the common-wealth.*

§. 133. By *common-wealth*, I must be understood all along to mean, not a democracy, or any form of government, but *any independent community*, which the *Latines* signified by the word *civitas*, to which the word which best answers in our language, is *common-wealth*, and most properly expresses such a society of men, which community or city in *English* does not; for there may be subordinate communities in a government; and city amongst us has a quite different notion from common-wealth: and therefore, to avoid ambiguity, I crave leave to use the word *common-wealth* in that sense, in which I find it used by king *James the first*; and I take it to be its genuine signification; which if any body dislike, I consent with him to change it for a better.

CHAP. XI.

OF THE EXTENT OF THE LEGISLATIVE POWER.

§ 134. THE great end of men's entering into society, being the enjoyment of their properties in peace and safety, and the great instrument and means of that being the laws established in that society; the *first and fundamental positive law* of all common-wealths *is the establishing of the legislative* power; as the *first and fundamental natural law,* which is to govern even the legislative itself, is the *preservation of the society,* and (as far as will consist with the public good) of every person in it. This *legislative* is not only the *supreme power* of the common-wealth, but sacred and unalterable in the hands where the community have once placed it; nor can any edict of any body else, in what form soever conceived, or by what power soever backed, have the force and obligation of a *law,* which has not its *sanction* from that *legislative* which the public has chosen and appointed: for without this the law could not have that, which is absolutely necessary to its being a *law, the consent of the society,* over whom no body can have a power to make laws, but by their own consent, and by authority received from them; and therefore all the *obedience,* which by the most solemn ties any one can be obliged to pay, ultimately terminates in this *supreme power,* and is directed by those laws which it enacts; nor can any oaths to any foreign power whatsoever, or any domestic subordinate power, discharge any member of the society from his *obedience to the legislative,* acting pursuant to their trust; nor oblige him to any obedience contrary to the laws so enacted, or farther than they do allow; it being ridiculous to imagine one can be tied ultimately to *obey* any *power* in the society, which is not the *supreme.*

§. 135. Though the *legislative,* whether placed in one or more, whether it be always in being, or only by intervals, though it be the *supreme* power in every common-wealth; yet,

First, It is *not,* nor can possibly be absolutely *arbitrary* over the lives and fortunes of the people: for it being but the joint power of every member of the society given up to that person, or assembly, which is legislator; it can be no more than those persons had in a state of nature before they entered into society, and gave up to the community: for no body can transfer to another more power than he has in himself; and no body has an absolute arbitrary power over himself, or over any other, to destroy his own life, or take away the life or property of another. A man, as has been proved, cannot subject himself to the arbitrary power of another; and having in the state of nature no arbitrary power over the life, liberty, or possession of another, but only so much as the law of nature gave him for the preservation of himself, and the rest of mankind; this is all he doth, or can give up to the common-wealth, and by it to *the legislative power*, so that the legislative can have no more than this. Their power, in the utmost bounds of it, is *limited to the public good* of the society. It is a power, that hath no other end but preservation and therefore can never have a right to destroy, enslave, or designedly to impoverish the subjects. The obligations of the law of nature cease not in society, but only in many cases are drawn closer, and have by human laws known penalties annexed to them, to inforce their observation. Thus the law of nature stands as an eternal rule to all men, *legislators* as well as others. The *rules* that they make for other men's actions, must, as well as their own and other men's actions, be conformable to the law of nature, *i.e.* to the will of God, of which that is a declaration, and the *fundamental law of nature being the preservation of mankind*, no human sanction can be good, or valid against it.

§. 136. *Secondly,* The *legislative,* or supreme authority, cannot assume to its self a power to rule by extemporary arbitrary decrees, but *is bound to dispense justice,* and decide the rights of the subject *by promulgated standing laws, and known authorized judges*: for the law of nature being unwritten, and so no where to be found but in the minds of men, they who through passion or interest shall miscite, or misapply it, cannot so easily be convinced of their mistake where there is no established judge: and so it serves not, as it ought, to determine the rights, and fence the properties of those that live under it, especially where every one is judge, interpreter, and executioner of it too, and that in his own case: and he that has right on his side, having ordinarily but his own single strength, hath not force enough to defend himself from injuries, or to punish delinquents. To avoid these inconveniences, which disorder men's properties in the state of nature, men unite into societies, that they may have the united strength of the whole to secure and defend their properties, and may have *standing rules* to bound it, by which every one may know what is his. To this end it is that men give up all their natural power to the society which they enter into, and the community put the legislative into the hands as they think fit, with this trust, that they shall be governed by *declared laws,* or else their peace, quiet, and property will still be at the same uncertainty, as it was in the state of nature.

§. 137. Absolute arbitrary power, or governing without *settled standing laws,* can neither of them consist with the ends of society and government, which men would not quit the freedom of the state of nature for, and tie themselves up under, were it not to preserve their lives, liberties and fortunes, and by *stated rules* of right and property to secure their peace and quiet. It cannot be supposed that they should intend, had they a power so to do, to give to any one, or more, an *absolute arbitrary power* over their persons and estates, and put a force into the magistrate's hand to execute his unlimited will arbitrarily upon them. This were to put themselves into a worse condition than the state of nature, wherein they had a liberty to defend their right against the injuries of others, and were upon equal terms of force to maintain it, whether invaded by a single man, or many in combination. Whereas by supposing they have given up themselves to the *absolute arbitrary power* and will of a legislator, they have disarmed themselves, and armed him, to make a prey of them when he pleases; he being in a much worse condition, who is exposed to the arbitrary power of one man, who has the command of 100,000, than he that is exposed to the arbitrary power of 100,000 single men; no body being secure, that his will, who has such a command, is better than that of other men, though his force be 100,000 times stronger. And therefore, whatever form the common-wealth is under, the ruling power ought to govern by *declared* and *received laws,* and not by extemporary dictates and undetermined resolutions: for then mankind will be in far worse condition than in the state of nature, if they shall have armed one, or a few men with the joint power of a multitude, to force them to obey at pleasure the exorbitant and unlimited decrees of their sudden thoughts, or unrestrained, and till that moment unknown wills, without having any measures set down which may guide and justify their actions: for all the power the government has, being only for the good of the society, as it ought not to be *arbitrary* and at pleasure, so it ought to be exercised by *established and promulgated laws;* that both the people may know their duty, and be safe and secure within the limits of the law; and the rulers too kept within their bounds, and not be tempted, by the power they have in their hands, to employ it to such purposes, and by such measures, as they would not have known, and own not willingly.

§. 138. *Thirdly,* The *supreme power cannot take* from any man any part of his *property* without his own consent: for the preservation of property being the end of government, and that for which men enter into society, it necessarily supposes and requires, that the people should *have property,* without which they must be supposed to lose that, by entering into society, which was the end for which they entered into it; too gross an absurdity for any man to own. *Men* therefore *in society having property,* they have such a right to the goods, which by the law of the community are their's, that no body hath a right to take their substance or any part of it from them, without their own consent: without this they have no *property* at all; for I have truly no *property* in that, which another can by right take from me, when he pleases, against my consent. Hence it is a mistake to think, that the *supreme* or *legislative power* of any common-wealth, can do what it will, and dispose of the estates of the subject *arbitrarily,* or take any part of them at pleasure. This is not much to be feared in governments where the *legislative* consists, wholly or in part, in assemblies which are variable, whose members, upon the dissolution of the assembly, are subjects under the common laws of their country, equally with the rest. But in governments, where the *legislative* is in one lasting assembly always in being, or in one man, as in absolute monarchies, there is danger still, that they will think themselves to have a distinct interest from the rest of the community; and so will be apt to increase their own riches and power, by taking what they think fit from the people: for a man's *property* is not at all secure, tho' there be good and equitable laws to set the bounds of it between him and his fellow subjects, if he who commands those subjects have power to take from any private man, what part he pleases of his *property,* and use and dispose of it as he thinks good.

§. 139. But *government,* into whatsoever hands it is put, being, as I have before shewed, intrusted with this condition, and for *this end,* that men might have and secure their *properties;* the prince, or senate, however it may have power to make laws, for the regulating of *property* between the subjects one amongst another, yet can never have a power to take to themselves the whole, or any part of the subjects *property,* without their own consent: for this would be in effect to leave them no *property* at all. And to let us see, that even *absolute power*, where it is necessary, is *not arbitrary* by being absolute, but is still limited by that reason, and confined to those ends, which required it in some cases to be absolute, we need look no farther than the common practice of martial discipline: for the preservation of the army, and in it of the whole common-wealth, requires an *absolute obedience* to the command of every superior officer, and it is justly death to disobey or dispute the most dangerous or unreasonable of them; but yet we see, that neither the serjeant, that could command a soldier to march up to the mouth of a cannon, or stand in a breach, where he is almost sure to perish, can command that soldier to give him one penny of his money; nor the *general*, that can condemn him to death for deserting his post, or for not obeying the most desperate orders, can yet, with all his *absolute power* of life and death, dispose of one farthing of that soldier's estate, or seize one jot of his goods; whom yet he can command any thing, and hang for the least disobedience; because such a blind obedience is necessary to that end, for which the commander has his power, *viz.* the preservation of the rest; but the disposing of his goods has nothing to do with it.

§. 140. It is true, governments cannot be supported without great charge, and it is fit every one who enjoys his share of the protection, should pay out of his estate his proportion for the maintenance of it. But still it must be with his own consent, *i.e.* the consent of the majority, giving it either by themselves, or their representatives chosen by them: for if any one shall claim a *power to lay* and levy *taxes* on the people, by his own authority, and without such consent of the people, he thereby invades the *fundamental law of property*, and subverts the end of government: for what property have I in that, which another may by right take, when he pleases, to himself?

§. 141. *Fourthly*, The *legislative cannot transfer the power of making laws* to any other hands: for it being but a delegated power from the people, they who have it cannot pass it over to others. The people alone can appoint the form of the common-wealth; which is by constituting the legislative, and appointing in whose hands that shall be. And when the people have said, We will submit to rules, and be governed by *laws* made by such men, and in such forms, no body else can say other men shall make *laws* for them; nor can the people be bound by any *laws*, but such as are enacted by those whom they have chosen, and authorized to make *laws* for them. The power of the *legislative*, being derived from the people by a positive voluntary grant and institution, can be no other than what that positive grant conveyed, which being only to make *laws*, and not to make *legislators*, the *legislative* can have no power to transfer their authority of making *laws*, and place it in other hands.

§. 142. These are the *bounds* which the trust, that is put in them by the society, and the law of God and nature, have *set to the legislative* power of every common-wealth, in all forms of government.

First, They are to govern by *promulgated established laws*, not to be varied in particular cases, but to have one rule for rich and poor, for the favourite at court, and the country man at plough.

Secondly, These *laws* also ought to be designed for no other end ultimately but *the good of the people*.

Thirdly, They must *not raise taxes* on the *property of the people, without the consent of the people*, given by themselves, or their deputies. And this properly concerns only such governments where the *legislative* is always in being, or at least where the people have not reserved any part of the legislative to deputies, to be from time to time chosen by themselves.

Fourthly, The *legislative* neither must *nor can transfer the power of making laws* to any body else, or place it any where, but where the people have.

Discussion Questions

1. What is the importance of private property within Locke's theory of government?

2. How does Locke imagine that his ideal commonwealth will be governed?

Sources

John Locke, *Second Treatise of Government*, ed. C.B. Macpherson, Indianapolis and Cambridge: Hackett Publishing Company, 1980.

D.A. Lloyd Thomas, *Locke on Government*, London: Routledge, 1995.

CHAPTER 14

Baron de Montesquieu
The Persian Letters

Rousseau
The Social Contract

MONTESQUIEU, *THE PERSIAN LETTERS*

Born in 1698 to a provincial aristocratic family, Montesquieu was sent to study outside of Paris at an institution renowned for its liberal and innovative curriculum before returning to Bordeaux in 1705 to study law. He moved to Paris a few years later, where he began to make the acquaintance of the leading literary and scientific figures of the time. Montesquieu showed the manuscript of *The Persian Letters* to his friend and mentor, Desmolets, in 1720. Desmolet cautioned Montesquieu about the repercussions of publishing it, but assured the young writer that it would sell. Anonymously published in Amsterdam a year later, the work instantly won fame and notoriety in France. Montesquieu, although he refused to admit his authorship, was soon recognized as having penned the letters. He became a coveted attendee of Paris' most famed intellectual salons and clubs and enjoyed the recognition of these circles and France's leading academic institutions throughout his life. He wrote another masterpiece a few years before his death, *The Spirit of the Laws*, in which he advocated relativistic political systems based on a country's geography, economy, and culture.

The Persian Letters narrates the adventures of two Persian travelers who journey to France and remain there between the years of 1711 and 1720. The two main characters discuss their impressions of Parisian life, often making biting criticisms of French society, religion, and customs. The book reflects the interest of Europeans in travel and exotic locations generated by the discovery of the New World, yet Montesquieu turned the typical travelogue on its head by making France the foreign and exotic focus of investigation. This innovation, along with the letter format, permitted Montesquieu to interrogate the most pressing philosophical concerns of Europeans in the early eighteenth century. Montesquieu was writing before the Enlightenment thinkers began to fully question the compatibility of scientific, rational thought and religion. However, the climate of religious intolerance that he had witnessed led him to level harsh criticisms against the Catholic Church and the king's policies. In the letters below, Montesquieu uses a critique of Islam to question the arbitrary nature of religious rules and the persecution of other faiths. He subtly rails against the revocation of the Edict of Nantes by Louis XIV in the last of the following letters by condemning the expulsion of various peoples from the Persian empire.

THE PERSIAN LETTERS

Montesquieu

LETTER XXIX

Rica to Ibben, at Smyrna

The pope is the head of the Christians; he is an old idol, revered by custom. At one time he was formidable even to princes, for he deposed them as readily as our magnificent sultans depose kings of Irimetta or Georgia. But they no longer fear him. He proclaims himself as the successor of one of the first Christians, called St. Peter; and it is a rich succession indeed, for he has immense treasures and a large country under his rule.

The bishops are administrators subordinate to him, and they have, under his authority, two very different functions. When assembled together they make, as he does, articles of faith. As individuals, their only function is to dispense with obedience to the law. For you should know that the Christian religion is burdened with a multitude of practices very difficult to follow, and as it is judged harder to fulfill these duties than to have bishops to dispense with them, the latter course has been followed in the interest of public utility. So, if someone does not wish to observe the Rhamazan, or prefers not to subject himself to the formalities of marriage, or wishes to break his vows, or to marry within prohibited bans, or sometimes even to get release from an oath, he has only to go to the bishop or the pope, who immediately grants dispensation.

The bishops do not make articles of faith of their own accord. There are multitudes of doctors, dervishes for the most part, who raise among themselves thousands of new religious questions; they are allowed to dispute for a long time, and the quarrel lasts until a decision comes to terminate it.

I can also assure you that there has never been a realm so prone to civil wars as that of Christ.

Those who publicize some novel proposition are at first called heretics. Each heresy is given a name, which is a rallying cry for those supporting it. But no one is a heretic unless he wishes to be, for he needs only to split the difference and to offer some subtle distinction to his accusers, and no matter what the distinction is, or whether it is intelligible or not, it renders a man pure as snow and worthy of being called orthodox.

What I have said is good only for France and Germany, for I have heard that in Spain and Portugal there are dervishes who do not understand a joke, and who have a man burned as if he were straw. Whoever falls into the hands of these men is fortunate only if he has always prayed to God with little bits of wood in hand, has worn two bits of cloth attached to two ribbons, and has sometimes been in a province called Galicia! Otherwise, the poor devil is really in trouble. Even though he swears like a pagan that he is orthodox, they may not agree, and burn him for a heretic. It is useless for him to submit distinctions, for he will be in ashes before they even consider giving him a hearing.

Other judges presume the innocence of the accused; these always presume him guilty. In doubt they hold to the rule of inclining to severity, evidently because they consider mankind as evil. On the other hand, however, they hold such a high opinion of men that they judge them incapable of lying, for they accept testimony from deadly enemies, notorious women, and people living by some infamous profession. In passing sentence, the judges pay those condemned a little compliment, telling them that they are sorry to see them so poorly dressed in their brimstone shirts, that the judges themselves are gentlemen who abhor bloodletting, and are in despair at having to condemn them. Then, to console themselves, they confiscate to their own profit all the possessions of these poor wretches.

Happy the land inhabited by the children of the prophets! There these sad spectacles are unknown. The holy religion brought by the angels trusts truth alone for its defense, and does not need these violent means for its preservation.

Paris, the 4th of the moon of Chalval, 1712

LETTER LXI

Usbek to Rhedi, at Venice

The other day, I went into a famous church called Notre Dame, and while I was admiring that superb edifice I had occasion to talk with an ecclesiastic who was also there out of curiosity. The conversation turned on the tranquillity of his profession. "Most people," he said to me, "envy the happiness of our condition", and they are right. However, there are some disadvantages, for although we are largely separated from the world, yet we are drawn into it on a thousand occasions. Thus we have a very difficult role to sustain.

"Worldly people are astonishing: they can suffer neither our censure nor our praise. If we try to reform them, they find us ridiculous; but if we approve, they regard us as men out of character. Nothing is as humiliating as the thought that you are scandalizing even the impious. And so we are obliged to be equivocal and to influence the libertines not by consistent action but by making them uncertain about how we will receive their observations. This requires great ability; the state of neutrality is a hard one. Worldly people who risk everything, who give in to all fancies, who follow or abandon them as they are successful or not, fare much better."

"And this is not all. We cannot maintain in the world that happy and peaceful way of life which everyone considers so desirable. As soon as we appear, we are forced into dispute. We are asked, for instance, to prove the value of prayer to a man who does not believe in God, or the necessity of fasting to someone who has always denied the immortality of the soul; the task is laborious, and there is no laughter on our side. Furthermore, we are constantly tormented by a desire to convert others to our opinions, for this is, as it were, the essence of our profession; yet it is as ridiculous as if Europeans worked to improve human nature by bleaching the skin of the Africans. We disturb the state and torment ourselves by trying to establish religious doctrines which are not at all fundamental; we resemble that conqueror of China who drove his subjects to revolt by insisting that they cut their hair and fingernails."

"There is danger even in our zeal to enforce the duties of our holy religion among those for whom we are responsible, and it cannot be accompanied by too much prudence. An emperor named Theodosius once put to the sword every inhabitant of a city, even the women and children. Appearing shortly afterward before a church, he found that a bishop named Ambrose had closed the doors to him as a sacrilegious murderer. That was a heroic action. But when the emperor, having finally made the penance that his crime required, was later admitted to the church and went to sit among the priests, that same bishop made him sit elsewhere. And that was the action of a fanatic, for in truth, excessive zeal should be avoided. What difference did it make either to religion or to the state whether this prince had or had not a place among the priests?"

Paris, the 1st of the moon of Rebiab I, 1714

LETTER LXXV

Usbek to Rhedi, at Venice

I must admit that I have not noticed among the Christians that lively faith in their religion which one finds in Mussulmans. With them there are great distances from profession to belief, from belief to conviction, and from conviction to practice. Their religion is less a subject of sanctification than a subject for dispute, which is open to everyone. Courtiers, soldiers, even women rise up against ecclesiastics, demanding that they prove to them what they have resolved not to believe. It is not that they have rationally so decided, or that they have taken the trouble to examine the truth or falsehood of the religion they reject; rather they are rebels, who have felt the yoke and thrown it off before learning what it is. Moreover, they are no more firm in their incredulity than in their faith; they live in an ebb and flow which carries them constantly between belief and disbelief. One of them once told me: "I believe in the immortality of the soul in periods of six months. My opinions depend entirely upon my body's constitution. According to the level of my animal spirits, the adequacy of my digestion, the rarity or heaviness of the air I breathe, or the solidity of the food I eat, I am alternately a Spinozist, a Socinian, a Catholic, an unbeliever, or a zealot. When the physician is close to my bed, the confessor has an advantage on me. I easily prevent religion from afflicting me when I am well, but I permit it to console me when I am ill. When I possess nothing more of earthly hope, religion comes and seizes me with its promises; I am pleased to surrender to it and to die on the side of hope."

Long ago the Christian princes freed all the slaves in their realms, because they said Christianity makes all men equal. It is true that this religious act was very useful to them, for by it they lessened the power of the nobles over the common people. Since then they have conquered lands where they have seen it was to their advantage to hold slaves, whom they have permitted to be bought and sold, forgetting that religious principle which once so deeply affected them. What can I say about this? The truth of one time is the error of another. Why should we not act like Christians? We were foolish to refuse settlements and easy conquests in pleasant climates, only because the water there was not sufficiently pure for bathing according to the dictates of the sacred Koran.

I give thanks to the all-powerful God, who sent his great prophet Hali, that I profess a religion which transcends all human interests and is as pure as the heavens from which it descended.

Paris, the 13th of the moon of Saphar, 1715

LETTER LXXXV

Usbek to Mirza, at Ispahan

You know, Mirza, that certain ministers of Shah Soliman formed the plan of requiring all Armenians in Persia either to leave the kingdom or become Mohammedans, thinking that our empire would remain polluted so long as it kept these infidels in its bosom.

That would have been the end of Persian greatness, had the counsels of blind devotion won out on that occasion.

It is not known how the project failed. Neither those who made the proposal, nor those who rejected it, realized the consequence of their decision; chance assumed the office of reason and policy and saved the empire from a peril greater than would have resulted from the loss of a battle and the capture of two cities.

By proscribing the Armenians, it is calculated that all the merchants and most of the country's artisans would have been wiped out in a single day. I am sure that the great Shah Abbas would rather have cut off both his arms than sign such an order; in exiling to the lands of the Mogul and the other Indian kings his most industrious subjects, he would have felt that he was giving them half of his realm.

The persecution of the Guebres by our zealous Mohammedans has forced them to leave in crowds for India and has deprived Persia of a hardworking people which, by its labor alone, was close to victory over the sterility of our soil.

Yet there remained to fanaticism a second blow to strike, that against our industry. The result was that the empire fell from within, bringing down with it, as a necessary consequence, that very religion which the zealots wished to strengthen.

If unprejudiced discussion were possible, I am not sure, Mirza, that it would not be a good thing for a state to contain several religions.

It is noticed that members of tolerated religions usually render more service to their country than do those of the dominant religion, because, cut off from the customary honors, they can distinguish themselves only by an opulence and wealth acquired by their labor alone, and often in the most difficult professions.

Furthermore, since all religions contain precepts that are socially useful, it is well that they be zealously observed; and what is better able to animate that zeal than a multiplicity of religions?

They are rivals who pardon nothing, and their jealousy extends to individuals. Each holds himself on guard, fearful of doing something which might dishonor his sect and expose it to the scorn and unpardonable censures of the other group.

Also, it is often observed that the introduction of a new sect into a state is the surest way to correct abuses in the old.

It is vain to say that it is not in the prince's interest to tolerate various religions in his realm. All the sects of the world assembled together would bring him no harm, for there is not one of them that does not prescribe obedience and preach submission.

I admit that history is filled with religious wars, but let us be careful here, for it is not the multiplicity of religions which has produced these wars, but the spirit of intolerance stirring those who believed themselves to be in a dominant position.

This is the proselytizing spirit which the Jews caught from the Egyptians, and which has passed from them, like a common epidemic disease, to the Mohammedans and Christians.

It is, in short, a kind of madness, the progress of which can be regarded only as a total. eclipse of human reason.

Finally, even if it were not inhumane to afflict another's conscience, and even if there did not result from such an act those bad effects which spring up by the thousands, it would still be foolish to advise it. Whoever would have me change my religion doubtlessly acts as he does because he would not change his, however he was forced; yet he finds it strange that I will not do something which he would not do himself, perhaps for the entire world.

Paris, the 26th of the moon of Gemmadi I, 1715

Discussion Questions

1. What kind of ideals does Montesquieu propose in place of the religious hypocrisy that he deplores?

2. What, in Montesquieu's view, are the consequences of policies of religious persecution and expulsion for the Persian empire, and implicitly, France?

Source

Montesquieu, *The Persian Letters*, trans. George R. Healy, Indianapolis and Cambridge: Hackett Publishing Company, 1999.

Peter V. Conroy, Jr., *Montesquieu Revisited*, New York: Twayne Publishers, 1992.

ROUSSEAU, *THE SOCIAL CONTRACT*

Born in 1712 to a French protestant family in Geneva, the death of his mother and the exile of his father marked Rousseau for life. In 1728, Rousseau himself left the city rather than the face punishment for a petty offense, and found romance and refuge in the house of Madame de Warens in Annency, France. His departure from Geneva marked the beginning of a life-long struggle find steady employment and emotional fulfillment. He worked as a servant, a tutor, a music transcriber and a writer, and constantly sought the companionship and patronage of wealthy, older women. Possessed of a difficult temperament and plagued by insecurity, Rousseau frequently argued with his patrons and broke with friends. He also fathered several children with a poor and uneducated servant woman, all of whom he sent to an orphanage, claiming that the state was better equipped than he to raise them.

Around 1745, Rousseau began to earn recognition for his work. He had received little formal education during his youth in Geneva and instead, schooled himself under the tutelage of his first patroness, Madame de Warens. After moving to Paris, he met Diderot, who in turn introduced the young philosopher to Parisian intellectual life. Rousseau contributed several entries on music to Diderot's *Encyclopedia* while he continued his studies, turning to political theory. However, rather than embrace the currents of thought so popular among the leading intellectuals of French society, Rousseau attacked Enlightenment ideals in an essay competition that won him immediate recognition. He published other works, among them a comic opera and several other entries in the *Encyclopedia*. By the mid-1750s, Rousseau was writing *The Social Contract*. In the meantime, relationships with patronesses and peers foundered, and Rousseau broke with Diderot, Grimm, Voltaire, and others. With the publication of *The Social Contract* and *Emile* in 1762, Rousseau was forced into exile. Rousseau ended his life in poverty, writing feverishly to justify his ideas until his death in 1778.

In *The Social Contract*, Rousseau considered the relationship between individuals and the state. Arguing that people must relinquish their individual liberties for the good of society as a whole, Rousseau left open-ended how the ideal society would govern itself, opening his work to diverse interpretations. Rousseau also attacked the notion of representative democracy, preferring more direct participation. In the passages below, Rousseau explores the nature of the social compact, the sovereign, and the civil state.

THE SOCIAL CONTRACT

Jean Jacques Rousseau

Let us assume that men have reached the point where the obstacles to their self-preservation in the state of nature are too great to be overcome by the forces each individual is capable of exerting to maintain himself in that state. This original state can then no longer continue; and the human race would perish if it did not change its mode of existence.

Now, since men cannot engender new forces, but can only combine and direct those already in existence, their only means of self-preservation is to form by aggregation a sum of forces capable of overcoming all obstacles, to place these forces under common direction, and to make them act in concert.

This sum of forces can only arise from the concurrence of many; but the force and liberty of each man being the primary instruments of his own self-preservation, how can he pledge them without harming himself and neglecting the cares he owes his own person? This problem, in relation to my subject, may be expressed in the following terms: To find a form of association which defends and protects the person and property of each member with the whole force of the community, and where each, while joining with all the rest, still obeys no one but himself, and remains as free as before.' This is the fundamental problem to which the social contract provides the answer.

The clauses of this contract are so completely determined by the nature of the act that the slightest modification would render them null and void; so that, though they may never have been formally declared, they are everywhere the same, everywhere tacitly admitted and recognised, until the moment when the violation of the social compact causes each individual to recover his original rights, and to resume his natural liberty as he loses the conventional liberty for which he renounced it.

These clauses, rightly understood, can be reduced to the following only: the total alienation of each member, with all his rights, to the community as a whole. For, in the first place, since each gives himself entirely, the condition is equal for all; and since the condition is equal for all, it is in the interest of no one to make it burdensome to the rest.

Furthermore, since the alienation is made without reservations, the union is as perfect as possible, and no member has anything more to ask. For if the individuals retained certain rights, each, in the absence of any common superior capable of judging between him and the public, would be his own judge in certain matters, and would soon claim to be so in all; the state of nature would continue, and the association would necessarily become tyrannical or meaningless.

Finally, each individual, by giving himself to all, gives himself to no one; and since there is no member over whom you do not acquire the same rights that you give him over yourself, you gain the equivalent of all you lose, and greater force to preserve what you have.

If the social compact is stripped to its essentials, therefore, you will find that it can be reduced to the following terms: 'Each of us puts in common his person and all his powers under the supreme direction of the general will; and in our corporate capacity we receive each member as an indivisible part of the whole.'

In place of the private and particular person of each of the contracting parties, this act of association immediately produces an artificial and collective body, made up of as many members as there are voices in the assembly, and receiving from this same act its unity, its collective personality, its life and its will. The public person thus formed by the union of all the rest was formerly known as a *city,* and is now called a *republic* or *body politic;* when passive it is known to its members as the *state,* when active as the *sovereign,* and as a *power* when it is being compared with its fellows. The members are known collectively as the *people;* and individually they are called, as participants in the sovereign authority, *citizens,* and, as men owing obedience to the laws of the state, *subjects.* But these terms are often confused and mistaken for one another; it is enough to be able to distinguish between them when they are used with absolute accuracy.

THE SOVEREIGN

From the formula already given, it can be seen that the act of association involves a reciprocal engagement between the public and its individual members, and that each individual, by contracting, so to speak, with himself, finds himself under the following two-fold obligation: as a member of the sovereign to the individual members, and as a member of the state to the sovereign. But the principle of civil law which states that no one can make binding commitments to himself is not applicable in this case; for there is a great difference between assuming obligations towards yourself, and doing so toward a whole of which you are a part.

It is also to be observed that public deliberation which, because of the two-fold nature of their relationship, is able to obligate all subjects toward the sovereign, cannot, for the opposite reason, obligate the sovereign toward itself; and that in consequence it is contrary to the nature of the body politic for the sovereign to bind itself by a law it cannot break. Since its relationships can only be conceived under a single aspect, it remains in the position of an individual contracting with himself; from which it follows that there is not, and cannot be, any sort of fundamental law binding on the body of the people, not even the social contract. This does not mean that this body cannot perfectly well assume obligations toward others in so far as they do not deviate from this contract; for in relation to foreigners, it becomes a simple entity, an individual.

But the body politic or sovereign, since it owes its being solely to the sanctity of the contract, can never bind itself, even to foreigners, to do anything derogatory to this original act, such as to alienate some part of itself or to subject itself to another sovereign. To violate the act by which it exists would be to destroy itself; and that which is nothing produces nothing.

From the moment when a multitude is thus united as a body, no one of its members can be offended without attacking the body itself; still less can the body be offended without affecting its members. Thus duty and interest alike oblige the two contracting parties to assist one another; and the same individuals should try to combine all the advantages which depend on both aspects of this twofold relationship.

Now the sovereign, being composed merely of the individuals who are its members, has and can have no interest contrary to theirs; consequently the sovereign power has no need to guarantee the rights of its subjects, since it is impossible for the body to want to harm all its members; and we shall see later that it cannot harm any particular individual. The sovereign, by the very fact that it exists, is always everything it ought to be.

The same is not true, however, of the relation of the subjects to the sovereign; in spite of their common interests, there would be no assurance that they would fulfil their obligations unless means were found to guarantee their fidelity.

Actually each individual may, as a man, have a private will contrary to, or divergent from, the general will he has as a citizen. His particular interest may speak to him quite differently from the common interest; his existence, being naturally absolute and independent, may make him envisage his debt to the common cause as a gratuitous contribution, the loss of which will be less harmful to others than the payment is burdensome to himself; and regarding the artificial person of the state as a fictitious being, because it is not a man, he would like to enjoy the rights of a citizen without fulfilling the duties of a subject, an injustice which, if it became progressive, would be the ruin of the body politic.

In order, therefore, that the social compact may not be a meaningless formality, it includes the tacit agreement, which alone can give force to the rest, that anyone who refuses to obey the general will shall be forced to do so by the whole body; which means nothing more or less than that he will be forced to be free. For this is the condition which, by giving each citizen to his country, guarantees him against any form of personal dependence; it is the secret and the driving force of the political mechanism; and it alone gives legitimacy to civil obligations, which otherwise would be absurd, tyrannical, and subject to the gravest abuses.

THE CIVIL STATE

This passage from the natural to the civil state produces a very remarkable change in man, substituting justice for instinct as the guide to his conduct, and giving his actions the morality they previously lacked. Then only is it that the voice of duty takes the place of physical impulse, and law the place of appetite; and that man, who until then has thought only of himself, finds himself compelled to act on other principles, and to consult his reason before listening to his inclinations. Although in this state he loses many of his natural advantages, he gains so many in return, his faculties are exercised and developed, his ideas are broadened, his sentiments ennobled and his whole soul elevated to such an extent that if the abuses of this new condition did not often degrade him beneath his former state, he ought unceasingly to bless the happy moment which wrested him forever from it, and turned him from a stupid and limited animal into an intelligent being and a man.

Let us draw up the balance sheet in terms readily capable of comparison. What man loses by the social contract is his natural liberty, and an unlimited right to everything he wants and is capable of getting; what he gains is civil liberty, and the ownership of all he possesses. In order to make no mistake as to the balance of profit and loss, we must clearly distinguish between natural liberty, which has no other limit than the might of the individual, and civil liberty, which is limited by the general will; and between possession, which results merely from force or from the right of the first occupier, and property, which can only be founded on a positive title.

To the foregoing we might add that, along with the civil state, man acquires moral liberty, which alone makes him truly master of himself; for the impulse of mere appetite is slavery, and obedience to self-imposed law is liberty. But I have already said more than enough under this head, and the philosophic meaning of the word liberty is not my present subject.

Discussion Questions

1. What kinds of rights and obligations does Rousseau envision the individual would possess in an ideal society?

2. How would you characterize Rousseau's ideal society? Were his intentions to create a more democratic or a more authoritarian society?

Sources

Jean Jacques Rousseau, *Political Writings*, trans. Frederick Watkins, Madison: University of Wisconsin Press, 1953.

Robert Wokler, *Rousseau: A Very Short Introduction*, Oxford and New York: Oxford University Press, 2001.

CHAPTER 15

Frederick the Great

Anti-Machiavel

FREDERICK THE GREAT, *ANTI-MACHIAVEL*

Frederick, heir to the domains of the Hohenzollern family, was born in 1712. His difficult and brutal father, Frederick William I ascended to the throne of Prussia in 1713.

Frederick William instructed the tutor of his son, Jacques Egide Duhan, a Huguenot refugee from France, to educate his son in a manner that conformed to his Calvinist and militaristic mode of rule. The clever instructor gave the appearance of following his patron's instructions, but managed to introduce the young prince to the new ideas of humanism, rationality, and secularism that characterized Enlightenment thought. Frederick developed an aversion for his father's militarism and violence, all the while thirsting for more knowledge of the great thinkers of the time.

In his youth, Frederick struck up a correspondence with Voltaire, in which the French thinker and the future king debated the ideas of the Florentine statesman, Machiavelli. The prince confessed in a letter in 1739 that he had begun a commentary on Machiavelli's *Prince*. Machiavelli had been persecuted by the Medici family after they fell from power, and wrote the *Prince* to address questions of monarchical power and the best means by which to found and manage a monarchy. In his view, the successful monarch must disregard morals and act ruthlessly if necessary. Machiavelli suggested that political expediency, not accountability, led to successful rulers. He based his proposals upon a pessimistic view of human nature. People only acted to their own advantage, and required coercion to act in a manner that benefited society as a whole. Thus, the ruler must take on the responsibilities of enforcing the common good.

Frederick's critique, dubbed the *Anti-Machiavel* by Voltaire, refuted Machiavelli's notion of the self-serving individual. Frederick believed that human beings were both enlightened and reasonable. Monarchs, as the embodiment of this Enlightenment vision of humanity, should therefore rule rationally and benevolently. The sovereign ruler first and foremost served the people. Frederick's vision of sovereignty signaled the shift from rule by divine right to legitimate rule founded upon rationality and justice. In essence, Frederick formulated what would later be dubbed enlightened despotism. In passages below, Frederick objects to Machiavelli's glorification of tyranny, advancing instead an ideal model of a humane and responsible leader.

ANTI-MACHIAVEL

Frederick the Great

The most precious trust that is placed in the hands of princes is the life of their subjects. Their post gives them the power of condemning the guilty to death or of pardoning them. As supreme arbiters of justice, a word from their mouth sets in motion the sinister instruments of death and destruction or gives wing to the speedy agents of their graces bearing good news. But such absolute power demands circumspection, prudence, and wisdom if it is not to be abused.

Tyrants set no value on human life. Their position prevents them from sympathizing with misfortunes that they do not experience. They are short-sighted people who cannot see beyond the tip of their nose and do not notice the rest of humanity. Perhaps if they could sense the horror of the punishments that they have ordered, of the cruelties committed out of their sight, and of everything that accompanies an execution, their hearts would not be so hard as to continue renouncing humanity and their impassiveness so unnatural as not to be touched.

Good princes regard their unlimited power over human life as the heaviest burden of their crown. They know that they are men just like those whom they must judge. They know that wrongs, injustices, and injuries can be repaired in this world, but that a hasty death sentence is an irreparable evil. They opt for severity only to avoid a worse alternative, and they make these ghastly decisions only in desperate cases, like a man with a gangrened limb who would reluctantly resolve to have it amputated in order to save the rest of his body. It is thus only under the greatest necessity that a prince must extinguish the life of his subjects, and he must be extremely circumspect and scrupulous about it.

Machiavelli treats such grave, serious, and important things as trifles. Human life is nothing to him, and interest, his only god, is everything. He prefers cruelty to clemency, and he counsels those who have recently risen to sovereignty to be particularly indifferent to being reputed cruel.

It is executioners who place Machiavelli's heroes on the throne, and it is force and violence that maintains them there. Cesare Borgia is the refuge of this political thinker when he seeks for examples of cruelty just as *Telemachus* is for M. de Fénelon when he shows the way to virtue.

Machiavelli also cites some verses that Virgil puts into the mouth of Dido, but this citation is entirely out of context, for Virgil has Dido speak just as M. de Voltaire does with Jocasta in his *Oedipus*. A poet has his personages speak in terms that are appropriate to their character. The authority of Dido and Jocasta has no bearing on a political treatise, which requires examples of great and virtuous men.

One reflection will suffice to answer the author in short. It is that crimes have such a ghastly interconnection that one necessarily leads to another. Thus usurpation is followed by banishment, proscription, confiscation, and murder. I ask if it is not being awfully harsh and execrably ambitious to aspire to sovereignty in view of the crimes that must be committed in order to maintain it. I ask if any man's personal interest justifies making the innocent who are opposed to his usurpation perish and what is the charm of a crown besmirched with blood. These reflections would perhaps make little impression on Machiavelli, but I am convinced that the whole world is not as corrupt as he is.

The political thinker recommends, above all, rigor towards the troops. He opposes the indulgence of Scipio to the severity of Hannibal. He prefers the Carthaginian to the Roman and immediately concludes that cruelty is the foundation of the order, discipline, and triumphs of an army. Machiavelli is not acting in good faith here, for he chooses Scipio, the softest and flabbiest of all disciplinarians, so as to oppose him to Hannibal in arguing for cruelty. The political thinker eloquently contrasts it to the weakness of Scipio, whom he himself confesses that Cato called the corrupter of the Roman army; and he presumes to use the differing success of these two generals in order to decry clemency, which he confuses as usual with the vice of excessive goodness.

I admit that order cannot subsist in an army without severity, for how can libertines, debauchees, scoundrels, poltroons, rash, crude, and mechanical animals be retained in their duty if the fear of punishments did not in part restrain them?

All that I ask of Machiavelli on this subject is moderation. Let him realize that if the clemency of an honest man leads him to goodness, his wisdom no less leads him to rigor. But he uses his rigor like an able pilot. He does not cut down the mast or the rigging of his vessel unless he is forced to do so by the imminent danger of storm and tempest.

But Machiavelli has not yet exhausted his subject. I am now at his most captious, subtle, and dazzling argument. He says that a prince finds it more to his advantage to be feared than loved since most people are ungrateful, fickle, dissimulating, cowardly, and avaricious; that love is made fragile by the malice and baseness of mankind, whereas fear of punishment gives much better assurance that people will do their duty; and that men are masters of their goodwill but not of their fear, so that a prudent prince will depend on it above all else.

I answer that I do not deny that there are ungrateful and dissimulating men in the world. I do not deny that fear is sometimes very powerful, but I claim that any king whose policy has no other goal than to be feared will reign over slaves, that he can expect no great actions from his subjects—for everything that is done out of fear or timidity always bears its imprint—that a prince who has the gift of being loved will reign over hearts since his subjects find it convenient to have him as a master, and that there are many examples in history of great and beautiful actions being performed out of love and fidelity. I may add that the fashion for seditions and revolutions seems to have entirely passed in our days, there being no kingdom except for England where the king has the least cause to fear his people; and even in England, the king has nothing to fear unless he himself rouses the tempest.

I thus conclude that a cruel prince is in more danger of treason than an easy going one; since cruelty is unbearable and one soon tires of fearing it, and goodness is always lovable and no one ever tires of loving it.

It would thus be desirable for the happiness of the world if princes were good without being too indulgent, so that their goodness would be a virtue and not a weakness.

There is a difference between causing a stir in the world and acquiring glory. The vulgar, who cannot evaluate reputations, are easily seduced by appearances, confusing good actions with extraordinary ones, wealth with merit, and brilliance with solidity. Enlightened people judge quite differently. They are hard to please. They dissect great men like cadavers. They examine if their intentions were honest, if they were just, if they contributed to the good of mankind, and if they tempered their courage with wisdom. They judge effects by causes rather than the other way around. They are not dazzled by brilliant vices and find that only merit and virtue are worthy of glory.

What Machiavelli finds great and worthy of reputation is the false brilliance which takes in the vulgar. He caters to the taste of the vilest and lowest people, but it is as hard for him as it is for Molière to combine a trivial manner of thinking with the nobility and taste of upstanding people. Those who appreciate the *Misanthrope* are all the more contemptuous of Scapin.

This chapter of Machiavelli contains both good and bad things. I shall first evoke Machiavelli's errors, I shall confirm what he says that is good and praiseworthy, and I shall then venture my sentiments on some related subjects.

The author sets up Ferdinand of Aragon and Bernabò of Milan as models for those who would distinguish themselves through great undertakings and extraordinary actions. Machiavelli finds their secret in boldness of undertaking and rapidity of execution. This is great, I agree, but it is not laudable unless the undertaking is just. "You who take pride in exterminating thieves," said the Scythian ambassadors to Alexander, "you are the biggest thief on earth, for you have pillaged and sacked all the nations that you have conquered. If you are a god, you must do good to mortals and not despoil them. If you are a man, remember what you are."

Ferdinand of Aragon did not merely wage war, but he used religion to veil his designs. If this king was religious, he committed an enormous sacrilege by using the cause of God as a pretext for his fury. If he was an unbeliever, he was a sly impostor and a hypocrite who made the credulity of the people serve his ambition.

It is dangerous for a prince to accustom his subjects to fight for quibbles. This renders the clergy indirect masters of war and peace. The Western Empire owed its fall in part to religious quarrels, and we have seen in France under the last Valois the ghastly consequences of the spirit of fanaticism and false zeal. A sovereign, it seems to me, should not interfere in the religion of his people and should do his utmost to recall his clergy and subjects to a spirit of mildness and tolerance. This policy is not merely in accord with the spirit of the Gospel, which preaches only peace, humility, and charity, but it is also in conformity with the interest of princes; since by uprooting false zeal and fanaticism from their states, they remove the most dangerous stumbling block from their path and avoid the most fearful of shoals; for the fidelity and good will of the vulgar will not hold up against the furor of religion and the enthusiasm of fanaticism, which offers martyrdom and heaven itself to assassins as the reward of their crimes and punishments.

A sovereign could thus not display enough contempt for the frivolous disputes of priests, which are only disputes of words, and he cannot be too careful to suppress superstition and the religious fervor that results from it.

Machiavelli advances, in the second place, the example of Bernabó of Milan to suggest to princes that they must reward and punish in an exemplary manner, so that all their actions bear the imprint of grandeur. Generous princes will not lack for reputation, particularly when they are liberal from greatness of soul rather than from pride.

Kindness can make them greater than all the other virtues. Cicero told Caesar, "There is nothing greater in your fortune than the power to save so many citizens, nor more worthy of your kindness than the will to do it." Thus a prince should always underpunish offenses and overreward services.

But here is a contradiction. In this chapter the political doctor wants princes to honor their alliances, and in the eighteenth chapter he formally dispensed them from keeping their word. He is like a good story teller who tells everyone a different yarn.

If Machiavelli reasons badly on all of the above, he speaks well about princes not committing themselves lightly with more powerful princes who might ruin them.

This is what a great German prince, esteemed by friends and enemies alike, knew full well. The Swedes invaded his states while he had gone to the aid of the emperor against France on the lower Rhine. On receiving this news, his ministers counseled him to call the Tzar of Russia to his aid. But this penetrating prince answered that the Muscovites were like bears who, once they were unchained, would not be easy to rechain. He sought his own vengeance, and he had no reason to repent of it.

Were I living in the next century, I would assuredly extend this article with some appropriate reflections, but it is not for me to judge the conduct of modern princes; and in this world one must know when to keep his mouth shut.

The topic of neutrality is as well treated by Machiavelli as that of alliances. Experience has clearly demonstrated that a neutral prince exposes his country to injury from both belligerents, that his states become the theater of war, and that he has everything to lose and nothing to gain by neutrality.

There are two manners of self-aggrandizement for a sovereign. One is by conquest, as when a warrior prince extends the limits of his dominion by force of arms. The other is by activity, as when a hard working prince makes the arts and sciences flourish in his states, rendering them more powerful and civilized.

This whole book deals only with the first manner of self-aggrandizement. Let us say something for the second, which is more innocent, more just, and every bit as useful as the first. The arts most necessary to life are agriculture, commerce, and manufacturing. The sciences most uplifting to the human spirit are geometry, philosophy, astronomy, eloquence, poetry, and everything that goes under the name of fine arts.

Since every country is different, there are some whose strength lies in agriculture, others in vineyards, others in manufacturing, and others in commerce: these arts sometimes even prosper together in some countries.

The sovereigns who choose this mild and charming manner of becoming more powerful should study particularly the condition of their country, so as to see which arts would be most likely to flourish there with some encouragement. The French and Spanish have noticed that they were lacking in commerce and have sought for this reason to ruin that of the English. If France succeeds in ruining the commerce of England, this will increase its power more than the conquest of twenty cities and a thousand villages ever could; and England and Holland, the two most beautiful and richest countries in the world, would gradually perish, so to speak, of consumption.

Countries rich in grains or vines must observe two things: one is to clear all lands carefully so as to put every inch of soil to good use; the other is to concentrate on finding new markets, cheaper means of transport, and ways to lower prices.

As to manufactures of all kinds, they may be what is most useful and profitable to a state; since they provide for the needs and luxuries of the inhabitants while neighbors are obliged to pay a tribute to your industry. On the one hand, they prevent money from leaving the country; and on the other, they bring it in.

I have always been convinced that the lack of manufactures was the cause in part of the great migrations from the northern countries by the Goths and Vandals who so often invaded the South. In those remote times, the only art known in Sweden, Denmark, and in most of Germany was agriculture. Cultivable lands were divided among as many proprietors as they could feed.

But since the human race has always been very fertile in cold countries, there came to be twice as many inhabitants in a country as could subsist by cultivation, so that the younger sons of good families got together and, making a virtue out of necessity, ravaged other countries and dispossessed their masters. Thus we see in the history of the Eastern and of the Western Empire, that the barbarians ordinarily asked only for fields to cultivate so as to obtain their subsistence. The northern countries are no less populous today, but since luxury has wisely multiplied our needs, it has given rise to manufacturing and to all those arts that provide subsistence to entire peoples who would otherwise be obliged to seek for it elsewhere.

A wise sovereign must exploit these ways of making a state prosper to the fullest. The surest mark of a well governed and affluent country is if it gives birth to the fine arts and to the sciences. These are flowers which grow in rich soil and good weather, but die under adverse conditions.

Nothing makes a reign more illustrious than the arts that flourish under its wing. The age of Pericles is as famous for Phidias, Praxiteles, and so many other great men who lived in Athens as for the battles won by the Athenians. That of Augustus is better known for Cicero, Ovid, Horace, and Virgil than for the proscriptions of this cruel emperor, who, after all, owes much of his reputation to Horace's lyre. That of Louis the Great is more famous for the Corneilles, the Racines, the Molières, the Boileaus, the Descartes, the Coypels, the Le Bruns, and the Ramondons than by that overblown passage of the Rhine, by that siege of Mons to which Louis came in person, and by the battle of Turin, which M. de Marsin lost for the Duke d'Orléans by official order.

Kings honor humanity when they distinguish and reward those who honor it the most, and who may these be if not those superior minds who work at perfecting our knowledge, who devote themselves to the cult of truth, and who neglect material comforts in order to develop the art of thinking. These wise men who enlighten the world deserve to be its legislators.

Happy are the sovereigns who themselves cultivate the sciences, who think like Cicero, the Roman consul, liberator of his country, and father of eloquence: "Letters mold youth and constitute the charm of old age. They make our prosperity more brilliant, console us in adversity; and in our homes, in those of others, in voyages, in solitude, anytime, anywhere, they make for the mildness of life."

Lorenzo de Medici, the greatest man of his nation, was the pacifier of Italy and the restorer of the sciences. His probity won him the general confidence of all the princes. Marcus Aurelius; one of the greatest Roman emperors, was a successful warrior no less than a wise philosopher. He practiced the most austere morality as well as preached it. Let us finish with his words: "A king who is conducted by justice has the universe for his temple. Upstanding people are its priests and worshippers."

Discussion Questions

1. Why does Frederick object to Machiavelli's ideas about the methods of effective leadership?

2. How do Frederick's recommendations on kingship reveal his immersion in the ideals of the Enlightenment?

Sources

Frederick of Prussia, *The Refutation of Machiavelli's Prince or Anti-Machiavel*, trans. Paul Sonnino, Athens: Ohio University Press, 1981.

Giles MacDonogh, *Frederick the Great: A Life in Deed and Letters*, New York: St. Martin's Press, 1999.

CHAPTER 16

Mary Wollstonecraft

A Vindication of the Rights of Woman

Robespierre

"On the Abolition of the Death Penalty (May 30, 1791)" and "On the Action to be Taken Against Louis XVI (December 3, 1792)"

MARY WOLLSTONECRAFT, *A VINDICATION OF THE RIGHTS OF WOMAN*

Mary Wollstonecraft, born in 1759, has long been considered one of the founding voices of the feminist movement in the eighteenth century. Her writings on the condition of women derived as much from her personal experiences as from observations of the world around her. She encountered heartbreak and economic strife early in life, when her father squandered the family fortune. Wollstonecraft worked tirelessly to support her siblings, despite their own ineptitude and laziness. The loss of her companion Fanny Blood to childbirth in 1786 made Wollstonecraft begin to consider the particular dangers and difficulties that women faced. An affair with the American Gilbert Imlay left her further disillusioned when she discovered his infidelity. After a short-lived career as a governess, Wollstonecraft found work as a reader and translator. She began to publish in the late 1780s as the French revolution stirred emotions on the continent and in England. The rejection of her affections by the Italian poet Fuseli, and the round of criticisms fired at her upon the publication of her radical pamphlet *A Vindication of the Rights of Men*, inspired Wollstonecraft to tackle the issue of women's rights. She published *A Vindication of the Rights of Woman* in 1792, a pamphlet in which Wollstonecraft broke ground by linking the economic difficulties facing women to issues of political equality.

The Enlightenment, with its concerns about equality among men, had opened up the possibility for intellectuals to raise the question of equality between men and women. Yet most male writers who considered the subject believed that women were the weaker sex and resisted the idea that women were rational beings meriting political equality. Wollstonecraft challenged such notions by advocating equal education for women, which would permit women to assume their rightful position as equals to men in other realms. Wollstonecraft based her argument upon the grounds that both men and women possessed immortal souls that did not differ because of sex. Therefore, men and women shared equal capacities. At the same time, Wollstonecraft also pointed to the harsh economic realities that most women faced, especially because of motherhood. Wollstonecraft's *A Vindication* refuted Rousseau's biologically based notions of the sexes, which Rousseau used as justification for advocating separate systems of education for men and women. In the excerpt below, Wollstonecraft attacks the alleged weakness of women and contends that women deserve more meaningful educations.

A VINDICATION OF THE RIGHTS OF WOMEN

Mary Wollstonecraft

After considering the historic page, and viewing the living world with anxious solicitude, the most melancholy emotions of sorrowful indignation have depressed my spirits, and I have sighed when obliged to confess that either Nature has made a great difference between man and man, or that the civilisation which has hitherto taken place in the world has been very partial. I have turned over various books written on the subject of education, and patiently observed the conduct of parents and the management of schools; but what has been the result?—a profound conviction that the neglected education of my fellow-creatures is the wand source of the misery I deplore, and that women, in particular, are rendered weak and wretched by a variety of concurring causes, originating from one hasty conclusion. The conduct and manners of women, in fact, evidently prove that their minds are not in a healthy state; for, like the flowers which are planted in too rich a soil, strength and usefulness are sacrificed to beauty; and the flaunting leaves, after having pleased a fastidious eye, fade, disregarded on the stalk, long before the season when they ought to have arrived at maturity. One cause of this barren blooming I attribute to a false system of education, gathered from the books written on this subject by men who, considering females rather as women than human creatures, have been more anxious to make them alluring mistresses than affectionate wives and rational mothers; and the understanding of the sex has been so bubbled by this specious homage, that the civilised women of the present century, with a few exceptions, are only anxious to inspire love, when they ought to cherish a nobler ambition, by their abilities and virtues exact respect.

In a treatise, therefore, on female rights and manners, the works which have been particularly written for their improvement must not be overlooked, especially when it is asserted, in direct terms, that the minds of women are enfeebled by false refinement; that the books of instruction, written by men of genius, have had the same tendency as more frivolous productions; and that, in the true style of Mahometanism, they are treated as a kind of subordinate beings, and not as a part of the human species, when improvable reason is allowed to be the dignified distinction which raises men above the brute creation, and puts a natural sceptre in a feeble hand.

Yet, because I am a woman, I would not lead my readers to suppose that I mean violently to agitate the contested question respecting the quality or inferiority of the sex; but as the subject lies in my way, and I cannot pass it over without subjecting the main tendency of my reasoning to misconstruction, I shall stop a moment to deliver, in a few words, my opinion. In the government of the physical world it is observable that the female in point of strength is, in general, inferior to the male. This is the law of Nature; and it does not appear to be suspended or abrogated in favour of woman. A degree of physical superiority cannot, therefore, be denied, and it is a noble prerogative! But not content with this natural preeminence, men endeavour to sink us still lower, merely to render us alluring objects for a moment; and women, intoxicated by the adoration which men, under the influence of their senses, pay them, do not seek to obtain a durable interest in their hearts, or to become the friends of the fellow-creatures who find amusement in their society.

I am aware of an obvious inference. From every quarter have I heard exclamations against masculine women, but where are they to be found? If by this appellation men mean to inveigh against their ardour in hunting, shooting, and gaming, I shall most cordially join in the cry; but if it be against the imitation of manly virtues, or, more properly speaking, the attainment of those talents and virtues, the exercise of which ennobles the human character, and which raises females in the scale of animal being, when they are comprehensively termed mankind, all those who view them with a philosophic eye must, I should think, wish with me, that they may every day grow more and more masculine.

This discussion naturally divides the subject. I shall first consider women in the grand light of human creatures, who, in common with men, are placed on this earth to unfold their faculties; and afterwards I shall more particularly point out their peculiar designation.

I wish also to steer clear of an error which many respectable writers have fallen into; for the instruction which has hitherto been addressed to women, has rather been applicable to *ladies,* if the little indirect advice that is scattered through "Sandford Merton" be excepted;

but, addressing my sex in a firmer I pay particular attention to those in the middle class, use they appear to be in the most natural state. Perhaps seeds of false refinement, immorality, and vanity, have been shed by the great. Weak, artificial beings, raised above the common wants and affections of their race, in a premature unnatural manner, undermine the very foundation of virtue, and spread corruption through the whole mass of society! As a class of mankind they have the strongest claim pity; the education of the rich tends to render them vain and helpless, and the unfolding mind is not strengthened by the practice, of those duties which dignify the human character. They only live to amuse themselves, and by the same law which in Nature invariably produces certain effects, they soon only afford barren amusement.

But as I purpose taking a separate view of the different ranks of society, and of the moral character of women in each, this hint is for the present sufficient; and I have only alluded to the subject because it appears to me to be the very essence of an introduction to give a cursory account of the contents of the work it introduces

My own sex, I hope, will excuse me, if I treat them like rational creatures, instead of flattering their *fascinating* graces, and viewing them as if they were in a state of perpetual childhood, unable to stand alone. I earnestly wish to point out in what true dignity and human happiness consists. I wish to persuade women to endeavour to acquire strength, both of mind and body, and to convince them that the soft phrases, susceptibility of heart, delicacy of sentiment, and refinement taste, are almost synonymous with epithets of weakness, and those beings who are only the objects of pity, and that of love which has been termed its sister, will soon become objects of contempt.

Dismissing, then, those pretty feminine phrases, which the men condescendingly use to soften our slavish dependence, and weak elegancy of mind, exquisite sensibility, and sweet docility of manners, supposed to be the sexual characteristics of the weaker vessel, I wish to show that elegance is inferior to virtue, that the first object of laudable ambition is to obtain a character as a human being, regardless of the distinction of sex, and that secondary views should be brought to this simple touchstone.

This is a rough sketch of my plan; and should I express my conviction with the energetic emotions that I feel whenever I think of the subject, the dictates of experience and reflection will be felt by some of my readers. Animated by this important object, I shall disdain to cull my phrases or polish my style. I aim at being useful, and sincerity will render me unaffected; for, wishing rather to persuade by the force of my arguments than dazzle by the elegance of my language, I shall not waste my time in rounding periods, or in fabricating the turgid bombast of artificial feelings, which, coming from the head, never reach the heart. I shall be employed about things not words! and, anxious to render my sex more respectable members of society, I shall try to avoid that flowery diction which has slided from essays into novels, and from novels into familiar letters and conversation.

These pretty superlatives, dropping glibly from the tongue vitiate the taste, and create a kind of sickly delicacy that turns away from simple unadorned truth; and a deluge of false sentiments and overstretched feelings, stifling the natural emotions of the heart, render the domestic pleasures insipid, that ought to sweeten the exercise of those severe duties, which educate a rational and immortal being for a nobler field of action.

The education of women has of late been more attended to than formerly; yet they are still reckoned a frivolous sex, and ridiculed or pitied by the writers who endeavour by satire or instruction to improve them. It is acknowledged that they spend many of the first years of their lives in acquiring a smattering of accomplishments; meanwhile strength of body and mind are sacrificed to libertine notions of beauty, to the desire of establishing themselves—the ,only way women can rise in the world—by marriage. And this desire making mere animals; of them, when they marry they act as such children may be expected to act,—they dress, they paint, and nickname God's creatures. Surely these weak beings are only fit for a seraglio! Can they be expected to govern a family with judgment, or take care of the poor babes whom they bring into the world ?

If, then, it can be fairly deduced from the present conduct, of the sex, from the prevalent fondness for pleasure which takes place of ambition and those nobler passions that open and; enlarge the soul, that the instruction which women have hitherto received has only tended, with the constitution of civil society to render them insignificant objects of desire—mere propagators of fools!—if it can be proved that in aiming to accomplish them without cultivating their understandings, they are taken out of their sphere of duties, and made ridiculous and useless when The short-lived bloom of beauty is over[1], I presume that *rational* men will excuse me for endeavouring to persuade them to become more masculine and respectable.

Indeed the word masculine is only a bugbear; there is little reason to fear that women will acquire too much courage or fortitude, for their apparent inferiority with respect to bodily strength must render them in some degree dependent on men in the various relations of life; but why should it be increased by prejudices that give a sex to virtue, and confound simple truths with sensual reveries?

Women are, in fact, so much degraded by mistaken notions of female excellence, that I do not mean to add a paradox when I assert that this artificial weakness produces a propensity to tyrannise, and gives birth to cunning, the natural opponent of strength, which leads them to play off those contemptible infantine airs that undermine esteem even whilst they excite desire. Let men become more chaste and modest, and if women do not grow wiser in the same ratio, it will be clear that they have weaker understandings. It seems scarcely necessary to say that I now speak of the sex in general. Many individuals have more sense than their male relatives; and, as nothing preponderates where there is a constant struggle for an equilibrium without it has naturally more gravity, some women govern their husbands without degrading themselves, because intellect will always govern.

---

[1] A lively writer (I cannot recollect his name) asks what business women turned of forty have to do in the world?

Discussion Questions

1. How do men and women differ, according to Wollstonecraft? What abilities do the sexes share?

2. Why does Wollstonecraft criticize contemporary methods of educating women?

Sources

Mary Wollstonecraft, *The Rights of Woman*, London: J.M. Dent & Sons Ltd., 1929.

Janet Todd, *Mary Wollstonecraft: A Revolutionary Life*, London: Weidenfeld & Nicolson, 2000.

Robespierre, "On the Abolition of the Death Penalty (May 30, 1791)," and "On the Action to be Taken Against Louis XVI (December 3, 1792)"

Robespierre, one of the principal characters of the French revolution, remains controversial. He personified the spirit of the revolution and all its contradictions, and today, is most often remembered as a scapegoat for the atrocities committed in the name of the revolution during the Terror. Born in Arras into a family of lawyers in 1758, Robespierre won a scholarship at the age of eleven to study in Paris, where he excelled as a student. Robespierre then went home to Arras to practice law until he was elected deputy of the Third Estate. He returned to Paris to participate in the Estates General, which had been summoned to meet in the spring of 1789.

As the revolution gained momentum, so did Robespierre. He had manifested little in the way of revolutionary zeal until he became a deputy. Once in Paris, however, he joined the Breton Club, whose members were later known as the Jacobins. Robespierre initially opposed an armed revolt against the king, but led the radical Jacobins against the more conservative Girondins once the National Convention began to meet. However, the lawyer from the provinces cast off his moderate ideas as popular support for revolution grew. Robespierre soon embraced the radicalism embodied by the Paris Commune and led the movement to execute King Louis for treason. With the death of the king on January 21, 1793, Robespierre rode the wave of revolutionary fervor to prominence within the new government. He played a leading role in the Committee of Public Safety, which although it is primarily known for the bloody repression of internal resistance to the revolution, also curbed inflation and successfully coordinated matters of education, land, industry, and the army. The pinnacle of Robespierre's revolutionary career came when he was elected president of the Convention in June 1794. Mere months later,

Robespierre fell victim to his own policies of political terror. The Jacobins had failed to retain popular support by passing a number of measures regarding food prices. Meanwhile, their moderate allies in the National Assembly had also undergone a change of heart due to the Terror and economic hardships. Robespierre was executed on July 28, 1794 by order of the Convention itself.

Robespierre's transformation from a moderate to a radical accompanied the enthusiasms and exigencies of the revolution. Early on, he discouraged the use of the death penalty, yet he became the most vociferous proponent of the Terror, which used the guillotine to enforce the ideals of the revolution. In the two speeches below, in which he discusses the use of capital punishment, the contrast between his early political leanings and then the shift to more radical views becomes apparent.

ON THE ABOLITION OF THE DEATH PENALTY (MAY 30, 1791)[1]

Robespierre

The news having reached Argos that citizens had been condemned to death in the city of Athens, people flocked into the temples to beseech the gods to persuade the Athenians not to harbor such cruel and distressing thoughts. I have come to beg not the Deity but the legislators, who should be the voice and the interpreters of the eternal laws bequeathed by the gods to mortal man, to efface from our penal code the bloody laws that sanction judicial murder, laws which are repugnant to the Frenchmen's new way of life and to their new constitution. I wish to prove to them: first, that the death penalty is fundamentally unjust; secondly, that it is not the most effective of penalties and that, far from preventing crimes, it increases them.

If, outside civil society, a ferocious enemy comes to threaten my life or if, repulsed a score of times, he yet returns to ravage the field that my hands have tilled, since I can only match his strength with mine, I must either perish or kill him; and, if I do so, the law of natural defense will justify and approve my deed. But in civil society, where the force of all can be arrayed against one, what principle of justice will it invoke in putting him to death? What necessity can society plead for dispensing with it? A conqueror who puts his captured enemies to death is called a barbarian! A man who cuts the throat of a child that he can disarm and chastise is thought to be a monster. An accused man whom society condemns is for it nothing more than a conquered and powerless foe; in its presence, he is weaker than a child in that of a grown man.

And so, in the eyes of truth and justice, the scenes of death that society commands with so much ceremony are nothing but cowardly murders, solemn crimes committed according to legal procedures, not by individuals but by the nation at large. Do not be astonished at the

---

[1] From H. Morse Stephens, *The Principal Speeches of the Statesmen and Orators of the French Revolution 1789-1795* (Oxford, 1892), II, 299-304; trans. G. Rude.

cruelty, the extravagance of some of these laws. They are the work of a few tyrants; they are the chains with which they fetter the human race; they are the arms with which they subject them; they have been written down in letters of blood. "It is not permitted to put a Roman citizen to death." Such was the law passed by popular acclaim; but Sulla conquered and said: "All who have borne arms against me are worthy of death." Octavius and the companions of his crimes confirmed this law.

Under Tiberius, it was a capital offense to have praised Brutus. Caligula condemned those to death who were sacrilegious enough to undress before the Emperor's image. When tyranny had invented the crime of *lèse-majesté*, in cases where men had committed deeds which were either insignificant or heroic, who would have dared to suggest that their penalty should be other than death without himself incurring a charge of *lèse-majesté?*

When fanaticism, the monstrous progeny of ignorance and despotism, invented in turn the crime of divine *lèse-majesté*, when in its madness it conceived the notion of avenging God himself, was it not obliged to offer him blood and to put him on a level with the monsters who claimed to be cast in his image?

The death penalty is necessary, say the upholders of the barbarous old ritual; without it there is no sanction powerful enough to arrest crime. Who has told you so? Have you counted all the means whereby the penal laws can inflict pain on the human system? Alas, short of actual death, how much physical and moral agony may a man not suffer!

The will to live yields to pride, the most imperious of all the passions that possess the soul of man; the most terrible punishment that can be inflicted on man as a social being is to be publicly disgraced, which is the supreme mark of public execration. When the legislator may strike the citizen in so many places and by so many means, why should he feel reduced to resorting to the penalty of death? Punishments are not intended to torture the guilty, but to deter men from committing crimes from a fear of the consequences.

The legislator who prefers death and other atrocious penalties to the milder means that he has at his disposal outrages the sensibility of the public and deadens moral sentiment among the people he governs; he is like an unskilled tutor who, from his frequent resort to cruel punishment, brutalizes and degrades the spirit of his pupil; moreover, in seeking to overstretch the springs of government, he weakens them and wears them out.

The legislator who maintains this penalty is one who renounces the salutary principle which recognizes that the most effective means of repressing crime is to make the penalty fit the passion that engendered it and to punish the passion, as it were, in itself. He confuses every principle, he disturbs every relationship, and he deliberately thwarts the objects of the penal laws.

The death penalty is necessary, you say? If that is so, why have so many nations been able to do without it? By what chance have these nations come to possess the greatest wisdom, happiness and freedom? If the penalty of death is the most suited to prevent great crime, it must follow that crime has been less frequent among the peoples who have adopted it and been the most lavish in its use. But the opposite is the truth. Take the example of Japan. Nowhere have the death penalty and torture been so lavishly applied; and nowhere have crimes been so frequent and so atrocious. It would appear that the Japanese have set out to vie in ferocity with the barbarous laws that scourge and afflict them. Did the republics of Greece, in which punishments were moderate and the death penalty was either rarely used or was completely unknown, present a picture of more crime and less virtue than countries governed by laws of blood? Do you believe that Rome was stained by more crimes when, in the days of its glory, the Portian law had abolished the severe penalties imposed by the kings and emperors than it was at the time of Sulla, who revived them, or of the emperors who carried their severity to an excess that was worthy of their infamous tyranny? Has Russia been convulsed since the autocrat who rules her entirely suppressed the death penalty, as if she had wished, by this act of humanity and enlightenment, to atone for the crime of maintaining millions of men under the yoke of despotism?

Listen to the voice of reason and justice; it cries out to us that human judgments are never sure enough for society to be able to put to death a man who has been condemned by fellow men who share his fallibility. Even if you imagine the most perfect judicial system, even if you find the most upright and the most enlightened judges, you will still have to allow place for error or prejudice. Why deny yourselves the means to correct them? Why condemn yourselves to the impossibility of holding out a helping hand to those unjustly sentenced? What is the use of vain regrets or of the illusory reparation that you make to an empty shadow or of lifeless ashes? To deny a man the possibility to expiate his crime by repentance or virtuous deeds, pitilessly to shut him off from any return to virtue and self-esteem, to hasten to force him into his tomb while he is freshly stained by his crime; all this is to my mind the most horrible refinement of cruelty.

The legislator's first duty is to form and to preserve public morality, which is the source of all liberty and of all social well-being. When, in pursuit of a particular goal, he departs from this basic and general aim, he commits the most vulgar and the most disastrous of errors.

The laws must, therefore, always afford peoples the purest model of reason and justice. If for the august severity and the moderate calm that should distinguish them they substitute anger and vengeance; if they shed human blood that they have the power to prevent and that they have no right to shed at all; if they display before the people scenes of cruelty and corpses bruised by torture, then they pervert in the citizens' minds all idea of what is just and unjust, and they give rise within society to terrible prejudices which engender others in their turn. Man is no longer so sacred a concern, his dignity is rated of lesser worth when public authority sets little store by his life. The idea of murder inspires far less terror when the law itself sets the example of it for all to see. Horror of crime diminishes when its only punishment is by another crime. Beware of confusing the efficacy of punishment with its excessive severity: the one is fundamentally opposed to the other. Moderate laws win the support of all; savage laws provoke a general conspiracy.

It has been observed that in free countries crimes have been more rare and penalties less severe; the one follows logically from the other. Free countries are those in which the rights of man are respected and in which, in consequence, the laws are just. Wherever they outrage humanity by their excessive rigor, they afford the proof that in such countries the dignity of man and the rights of the citizen are unknown or are not respected and that the legislator is but a master in command of slaves, whom he pitilessly punishes according to his fancy. I conclude that the death penalty must be repealed.

ON THE ACTION TO BE TAKEN AGAINST LOUIS XVI (DECEMBER 3, 1792)[2]

Robespierre

The Assembly has been unwittingly dragged away from the real point at issue. It is not a question of conducting a trial. Louis is not an accused person; you are not judges; you are not, and you cannot be, anything else but statesmen and representatives of the nation. It is not a question of your passing a sentence for or against a man, but of taking a measure of public security and of performing an act of national policy. A dethroned king in a Republic is good for only two things: either to disturb the peace of the State and to overthrow liberty, or to confirm both peace and liberty. Now, I maintain the course of your deliberations has run directly counter to this latter aim. . . .

Louis was King; then the Republic was founded. The important question that is occupying you can be decided by these same few words. Louis was dethroned for his crimes. Louis denounced the French people as rebels. He called in the armies of his fellow tyrants, and the victory of the people decided that he alone was the rebel. Louis cannot be judged; he is already judged. He is condemned, or if he is not, the sovereignty of the Republic is not absolute. To propose a trial for Louis XVI, in whatever form, is to retrace our steps towards royal and constitutional despotism. It is a counterrevolutionary idea, since it puts the Revolution itself on trial. If Louis can still be the subject of a trial, Louis can be absolved, he can be judged innocent. . . . Citizens, take care. You are being deceived by false notions. You are confusing the rules of civil and positive law with the principles of the law of nations. You are confusing the mutual relationships of citizens with the relationship of a nation with an enemy conspiring against it. You are confusing the situation of a people in revolution with that of a people with a settled government. You are confusing a nation punishing a public official with one that is destroying the government itself. . . .

---

[2] From H. Morse Stephens, *op. cit.* II, 358-66; trans. W.J. Gardner and G. Rude.

When a nation has been found to have recourse to the right of insurrection, it returns to a state of nature with regard to the tyrant. How can the latter invoke the social pact? He has destroyed it....It is a gross contradiction to suppose that the Constitution can preside over this new state of affairs. It would be to suppose that the Constitution itself has survived. What are the laws which now replace it? The laws of nature, that which is the basis of society itself: the safety of the people. The right of punishing the tyrant and the right of dethroning him are the same things. They do not take different forms. The trial of the tyrant is insurrection; his judgment is the fall of his power; his punishment is what the liberty of the people demands.

We have let ourselves be led into error by foreign examples that have nothing in common with us. Cromwell had Charles I tried by a court under his control, and Elizabeth had Mary of Scotland condemned in the same way. These methods are natural to tyrants sacrificing their equals, not to the people, but to their own ambition and seeking to mislead the opinions of the populace by shams. It was not then a question of principles or of liberty but of trickery and intrigues. But the people! What other law can they follow save that of justice and reason backed by their own supreme power?

We treat as legitimate acts what any free people would have regarded as the greatest of crimes. We ourselves incite the citizens to baseness and corruption. One day we may be giving civic crowns to Louis' defenders; for if they defend his cause, they have the right to hope for its triumph; otherwise, you would be performing a ridiculous comedy in the eyes of the world. And we dare speak of Republic! We invoke procedures because we have no principles; we pride ourselves on our moderation because we lack all energy; we display a false humanity because feelings of true humanity are foreign to us; we revere the shadow of a king because we are without compassion for the weak and oppressed.

Bring Louis XVI to trial! But what is this trial but the appeal of insurrection to some court of law or assembly? When a king has been destroyed by the people, who has the right to revive him and to make of him a new pretext for disorder and rebellion? And what other consequences might flow from such an action? By giving a platform to the champions of Louis XVI you reawaken all the quarrels of despotism with liberty; you accord the right to blaspheme against the Republic and against the people, for the right to defend the former despot carries with it the right to say anything that may promote his cause. You will rouse all the factions; you will reanimate and rekindle the dormant embers of royalism. One will be free to take sides for or against. What will be more legitimate and more natural than to repeat and spread abroad the maxims that his defenders will be able to profess aloud at your bar and from your very rostrum? What sort of Republic is it whose founders invite its enemies to come in from every side in order to attack it in its cradle? . . .

It is a great cause, it has been said, that must be judged with a slow and measured circumspection. It is you who make a great cause of it. Nay, more: it is you that make a cause of it at all. What is there great in it? Is it the complications? No. Is it the person concerned? In the eyes of freemen, there is none so vile; in the eyes of humanity, there is none more guilty. He can impress only those who are more cowardly than himself. Is it the usefulness of its result? All the greater is the reason to hasten it. A great cause would be the draft of a law in the people's interest, or the cause of a humble citizen oppressed by despotism. What is the motive for these eternal delays that you recommend to us? Do you fear to wound the feelings of the people? as if they feared anything other than the weakness or ambition of its mandatories? as if the people were a vile herd of slaves, stupidly attached to the stupid tyrant that it has proscribed, desiring, at whatever price, to wallow in baseness and servitude! You speak of opinion. Is it not your duty to guide it and to give it strength? If it is misled or becomes perverted, who should be blamed for it but you? Do you fear to incur the displeasure of the foreign kings who are leagued against us? You will not tell me that the way to defeat them is to appear to fear them and that the way to confound the criminal conspiracy of the European despots is to respect the person of their accomplice! Do you fear the peoples of other countries? If so, you still believe in their innate love of tyranny. Why then do you aspire to the glory of liberating the human race? What contradiction leads you to suppose that the nations that were not astonished by our proclamation of the rights of humanity will be appalled by the punishment of one of its most cruel oppressors? Or, it has been said, you fear the verdict of posterity? Yes, posterity will indeed be astonished by your weakness and inconsequence; and our descendants will laugh at both the presumption and the prejudices of their fathers.

It has been said that it would take genius to go to the roots of this question. I maintain that all that is needed is good faith: it is far less a matter of seeking enlightenment than of not deliberately seeking to be blinded. Why should what appears clear to us at one moment appear so obscure at another? Why should that which the good sense of the people so easily resolves be changed into an almost insoluble problem for its delegates? Have they the right to have a general will and a wisdom different from those prescribed by universal reason?

I have heard the defenders of inviolability advance a theory so bold that I would almost have hesitated to utter it myself. They have said that if the people had put Louis XVI to death on August 10, they would have committed a virtuous act. But such a view can have no other basis than the crimes of Louis XVI and the rights of the people. Has, then, a lapse of three months altered his crimes or the people's rights? If at that time he was saved from public indignation, it was no doubt solely in order that his punishment, when solemnly pronounced by the National Convention in the name of the nation, might make a deeper impression on the enemies of mankind; but now to raise doubts as to his guilt or to the propriety of bringing him to justice is to betray the solemn pledge given to the people of France. There are perhaps those who, either to prevent the Assembly from assuming a character worthy of itself, or to refuse to give the nations an example to inspire in them a love of republican principles, or for even less honourable motives, would weep no tears if a private hand were to usurp the duties of public justice. Citizens, beware of this trap; any man who dared to give such counsel would merely serve the enemies of the people. Whatever happens, Louis' punishment will serve no purpose unless it bear the solemn character of an act of public vengeance.

How should the people be concerned about the wretched person of the last of our kings? Representatives, what concerns them, and what concerns you, is that you should carry out the duties that their confidence imposes on you. You have proclaimed the Republic, but have you given it substance? We have not yet enacted a single law that is worthy of that name; we have not yet remedied a single abuse inherited from despotism. Remove the names, and tyranny is still entirely with us; moreover, we have factions more vile and charlatans more immoral, and we are threatened by new outbreaks of disorder and civil war. We are a Republic, and Louis still lives! and you still place the person of the King between ourselves and liberty! Let us beware, by an excess of scruple, of becoming criminals; let us beware that, by showing too great an indulgence for the culprit, we do not put ourselves in his place.

A new problem arises. To what punishment shall we sentence Louis? The death penalty is too cruel. No, says another, to live is more cruel; I demand that he should live. Advocates of Louis, is it from pity or from cruelty that you wish him to escape the penalty for his crimes? For myself, I abhor the penalty of death that your laws so liberally impose, and I have neither love nor hatred for the King; it is only crime that I hate. I demanded the abolition of the death penalty in the Assembly that you still call the Constituent Assembly; and it is not my fault if the first principles of reason appeared to that Assembly to be moral and political heresies. But if you never thought to invoke them on behalf of so many wretches whose crimes are not so much theirs as those of the government, what prompts you now to remember them in order to plead the cause of the greatest of all criminals? You ask for an exception to the penalty of death for the one man in whose case it would be justified! Yes, the death penalty in general is a crime, and for this one reason: that, according to the indestructible laws of nature, it can be justified only in cases where it is necessary for the security of the person or the State. Now, public security never warrants that it be invoked in respect of ordinary common-law offenses, because society can always prevent them by other means and render the culprit harmless to injure her further. But when a king is dethroned in the midst of a Revolution whose laws are still in the making, a king whose very name draws the scourge of war onto a nation in tumult, neither prison nor exile can destroy the influence that his existence continues to exert on the public welfare; and this cruel exception to the ordinary laws that justice prescribes can be imputed only to the nature of his crimes. It is with regret that I utter this baneful truth....But Louis must die in order that our country may live. Among a people at peace, free and respected both within and without its borders, one might heed the advice that you are given to be generous. But a people whose liberty, after so much sacrifice and struggle, is still in dispute; a people whose laws are still inexorable only for the weak and the poor; a people which is still divided by the crimes of tyranny; such a people desires to be avenged; and the generosity that we are called upon to display would be too much like that of a band of brigands sharing out their spoil.

I propose that you adopt a decree forthwith to determine Louis' fate. As for his wife, you will send her before the courts, like all other persons charged with similar crimes. His son will be kept in the Temple until peace and public liberty have been assured. In his own case, I demand that the Convention *declare him, forthwith, to be a traitor to the French nation and a criminal against humanity;* I demand that he be made a great example of before the whole world in the very place where, on August 10, the generous martyrs of liberty perished. I demand that this memorable event be consecrated by the erection of a monument, destined to nourish in the hearts of the peoples the love of their rights and the hatred of tyrants; and in the souls of tyrants a wholesome terror of popular justice.

Discussion Questions

1. In the first speech, why does Robespierre oppose capital punishment?
2. In the second speech, how does Robespierre justify the execution of the king?

Sources

George Rudé, ed., *Robespierre*, New Jersey: Prentice-Hall, 1967.

Colin Haydon and William Doyle, eds., *Robespierre*, Cambridge: Cambridge University Press, 1999.

CHAPTER 17

Malthus

An Essay on the Principle of Population

Adam Smith

The Wealth of Nations

MALTHUS, AN ESSAY ON THE PRINCIPLE OF POPULATION

Thomas Robert Malthus came of age during the French and Industrial Revolutions. Born in 1766, Malthus also witnessed the rise of secularism and the emergence of the modern sciences. His father, a gentleman, had known Hume and Rousseau, and endeavored to provide his son with a liberal education. Malthus entered Jesus College at Cambridge in 1784, where he excelled in many subjects, especially mathematics. He graduated with honors, and in 1793, was elected to a fellowship at the same institution. The publication of *An Essay on the Principle of Population* in 1798 furthered his academic career. In 1805, Malthus was honored with an appointment to the first professorship in political economy ever created, at the East India College. This institution, founded to train civil servants for Britain's expanding colony on the Indian subcontinent, employed Malthus until his death in 1834. His contributions to the new discipline of political economy were recognized through membership in the Royal Society, the Political Economy Club, the Royal Academy of Literature, the Statistical Society, and several international societies.

Despite the efforts of his tutors to convert him to their more radical views, Malthus remained a moderate throughout his life. His most renowned work, *An Essay on the Principle of Population*, challenged the progressive idealism of radical thinkers such as Godwin, the husband of Mary Wollstonecraft, and Condorcet, the French writer. Malthus argued that natural laws checked the advance of population growth. According to Malthus, the birth rate of humans would repeatedly outstrip the food supply, and result in famines or other curbs on an expanding population. His theory countered optimistic views that Europe's economic expansion could indefinitely sustain population growth. Malthus even dared to suggest that economic progress, by encouraging families to have more children, led to overpopulation and then crisis. In the passage below,

Malthus summarizes his theory, and then makes several recommendations regarding how to prevent the calamities that he gloomily predicted for the near future. He assigns individual responsibility for preventing such disasters, and in the process, reveals his moderate leanings.

AN ESSAY ON THE PRINCIPLE
OF POPULATION

Thomas Robert Malthus

CHAPTER I

OF MORAL RESTRAINT, AND OUR OBLIGATION TO
PRACTISE THIS VIRTUE

As it appears that in the actual state of every society which has come
within our review the natural progress of population has been constantly
and powerfully checked, and as it seems evident that no improved form
of government, no plans of emigration, no benevolent institution, and no
degree or direction of national industry can prevent the continued action
of a great check to population in some form or other, it follows that we
must submit to it as an inevitable law of nature; and the only inquiry that
remains is how it may take place with the least possible prejudice to the
virtue and happiness of human society.

All the immediate checks to population which have been observed
to prevail in the same and different countries seem to be resolvable
into moral restraint, vice, and misery; and if our choice be confined to
these three, we cannot long hesitate in our decision respecting which it
would be most eligible to encourage.

In the first edition of this essay I observed that as from the laws of
nature it appeared that some check to population must exist, it was
better that this check should arise from a foresight of the difficulties
attending a family and the fear of dependent poverty than from the
actual presence of want and sickness. This idea will admit of being
pursued farther; and I am inclined to think that from the prevailing
opinions respecting population, which undoubtedly originated in
barbarous ages, and have been continued and circulated by that part of
every community which may be supposed to be interested in their
support, we have been prevented from attending to the clear dictates of
reason and nature on this subject.

Natural and moral evil seem to be the instruments employed by the
Deity in admonishing us to avoid any mode of conduct which is not

suited to our being, and will consequently injure our happiness. If we are intemperate in eating and drinking, our health is disordered; if we indulge the transports of anger, we seldom fail to commit acts of which we afterwards repent; if we multiply too fast, we die miserably of poverty and contagious diseases. The laws of nature in all these cases are similar and uniform. They indicate to us that we have followed these impulses too far, so as to trench upon some other law, which equally demands attention. The uneasiness we feel from repletion, the injuries that we inflict on ourselves or others in anger, and the inconveniences we suffer on the approach of poverty, are all admonitions to us to regulate these impulses better; and if we heed not this admonition, we justly incur the penalty of our disobedience, and our sufferings operate as a warning to others.

From the inattention of mankind hitherto to the consequences of increasing too fast, it must be presumed that these consequences are not so immediately and powerfully connected with the conduct which leads to them as in the other instances; but the delayed knowledge of particular effects does not alter their nature, or our obligation to regulate our conduct accordingly, as soon as we are satisfied of what this conduct ought to be. In many other instances it has not been till after long and painful experience that the conduct most favourable to the happiness of man has been forced upon his attention. The kind of food and the mode of preparing it best suited to the purposes of nutrition and the gratification of the palate, the treatment and remedies of different disorders, the had effects on the human frame of low and marshy situations, the invention of the most convenient and comfortable clothing, the construction of good houses, and all the advantages and extended enjoyments which distinguish civilised life, were not pointed out to the attention of man at once, but were the slow and late result of experience and of the admonitions received by repeated failures.

Diseases have been generally considered as the inevitable inflictions of Providence, but perhaps a great part of them may more justly be considered as indications that we have offended against some of the laws of nature. The plague at Constantinople and in other towns of the East is a constant admonition of this kind to the inhabitants. The human constitution cannot support such a state of filth and torpor; and as dirt, squalid poverty, and indolence are in the highest degree unfavourable to happiness and virtue, it seems a benevolent dispensation that such a state should by the laws of nature produce disease and death as a beacon to others to avoid splitting on the same rock.

The prevalence of the plague in London till the year 1666 operated in a proper manner on the conduct of our ancestors; and the removal of nuisances, the construction of drains, the widening of the streets, and the giving more room and air to the houses, had the effect of eradicating completely this dreadful disorder, and of adding greatly to the health and happiness of the inhabitants.

In the history of every epidemic it has almost invariably been observed that the lower classes of people, whose food was poor and insufficient, and who lived crowded together in small and dirty houses, were the principal victims. In what other manner can Nature point out to us that, if we increase too fast for the means of subsistence so as to render it necessary for a considerable part of the society to live in this miserable manner, we have offended against one of her laws? This law she has declared exactly in the same manner as she declares that intemperance in eating and drinking will be followed by ill health, and that, however grateful it may be to us at the moment to indulge this propensity to excess, such indulgences will ultimately produce unhappiness. It is as much a law of nature that repletion is bad for the human frame, as that eating and drinking, unattended with this consequence, are good for it.

An implicit obedience to the impulses of our natural passions would lead us into the wildest and most fatal extravagances, and yet we have the strongest reasons for believing that all these passions are so necessary to our being that they could not be generally weakened or diminished without injuring our happiness. The most powerful and universal of all our desires is the desire of food, and of those things— such as clothing, houses, &c.—which are immediately necessary to relieve us from the pains of hunger and cold. It is acknowledged by all that these desires put in motion the greatest part of that activity from which the multiplied improvements and advantages of civilised life are derived, and that the pursuit of these objects and the gratification of these desires form the principal happiness of the larger half of mankind, civilised or uncivilised, and are indispensably necessary to the more refined enjoyments of the other half. We are all conscious of the inestimable benefits that we derive from these desires when directed in a certain manner, but we are equally conscious of the evils resulting from them when not directed in this manner—so much so that society has taken upon itself to punish most severely what it considers as an irregular gratification of them. And yet the desires in both cases are equally natural, and, abstractedly considered, equally virtuous. The act of the hungry man who satisfies his appetite by taking a loaf from the shelf of another is in no respect to be distinguished from the act of him who does the same thing with a loaf of his own, but by its consequences. From the consideration of these consequences we feel the most perfect conviction that if people were not prevented from gratifying their natural desires with the loaves in the possession of others, the number of loaves would universally diminish. This experience is the foundation of the laws relating to property, and of the distinctions of virtue and vice in the gratification of desires otherwise perfectly the same.

If the pleasure arising from the gratification of these propensities were universally diminished in vividness, violations of property would become less frequent ; but this advantage would be greatly overbalanced by the narrowing of the sources of enjoyment. The diminution in the quantity of all those productions which contribute to human gratification would be much greater in proportion than the diminution of thefts, and the loss of general happiness on the one side would be beyond comparison greater than the gain of happiness on the other. When we contemplate the constant and severe toils of the greatest part of mankind, it is impossible not to be forcibly impressed with the reflection that the sources of human happiness would be most cruelly diminished if the prospect of a good meal, a warm house, and a comfortable fireside in the evening were not incitements sufficiently vivid interest and cheerfulness to the labours and privations of the day.

After the desire of food, the most powerful and general of our desires is the passion between the sexes, taken in an enlarged sense. Of the happiness spread over human life by this passion very few are unconscious. Virtuous love, exalted by friendship, seems to be that sort of mixture of sensual and intellectual enjoyment, particularly suited to the nature of man, and most powerfully calculated to awaken the sympathies of the soul, and produce the most exquisite gratifications. Perhaps there is scarcely a man who has once experienced the genuine delight of virtuous love, however great his intellectual pleasures may have been, who does not look back to that period as the sunny spot in his whole life, where his imagination loves most to bask, which he recollects and contemplates with the fondest regret, and which he would wish to live over again. It has been said by Mr. Godwin, in order to show the evident inferiority of the pleasures of sense, "Strip the commerce of the sexes of all its attendant circumstances, and it would be generally despised." He might as well say to a man who admires trees, Strip them of their spreading branches and lovely foliage, and what beauty can you see in a bare pole? But it was the tree with the branches and foliage, and not without them, that excited admiration.

It is "the symmetry of person, the vivacity, the voluptuous softness of temper, the affectionate kindness of feeling, the imagination, and the wit" of a woman, which excites the passion of love, and not the mere distinction of her being a female.

It is a very great mistake to suppose that the passion between the sexes only operates and influences human conduct, when the immediate gratification of it is in contemplation. The formation and steady pursuit of some particular plan of life has been justly considered as one of the most permanent sources of happiness; but I am inclined to believe that there are not many of these plans formed which are not connected in a considerable degree with the prospect of the gratification of this passion, and with the support of children arising from it. The evening meal, the warm house, and the comfortable fireside would lose half their interest if we were to exclude the idea of some object of affection with whom they were to be shared.

We have also great reason to believe that the passion between the sexes has the most powerful tendency to soften and meliorate the human character, and keep it more alive to all the kindlier emotions of benevolence and pity. Observations on savage life have generally tended to prove that nations in which this passion appeared to be less vivid, were distinguished by a ferocious and malignant spirit, and particularly by tyranny and cruelty to the sex. If indeed this bond of conjugal affection were considerably weakened, it seems probable either that the man would make use of his superior physical strength, and turn his wife into a slave, as among the generality of savages, or at best that every little inequality of temper, which must necessarily occur between two persons, would produce a total alienation of affection; and this could hardly take place without a diminution of parental fondness and care, which would have the most fatal effect on the happiness of society.

It may be further remarked, and observations on the human character in different countries warrant us in the conclusion, that the passion is stronger, and its general effects in producing gentleness, kindness, and suavity of manners, much more powerful, where obstacles are thrown in the way of very early and universal gratification. In some of the southern countries, where every impulse may be almost immediately indulged, the passion sinks into mere animal desire, is soon weakened and almost extinguished by excess, and its influence on the character is extremely confined. But in European countries, where, though the women are not secluded, yet manners have imposed considerable restraints on this gratification, the passion not only rises in force, but in the universality and beneficial tendency of its effects; and has often the greatest influence in the formation and improvement of the character, where it is the least gratified.

Considering then the passion between the sexes in all its bearings and relations, and including the endearing engagement of parent and child resulting from it, few will be disposed to deny that it is one of the principle ingredients of human happiness. Yet experience teaches us that much evil flows from the irregular ratification of it; and though the evil be of little weight in the scale when compared with the good, yet its absolute quantity cannot be inconsiderable, on account of the strength and universality of the passion. It is evident however from the general conduct of all governments in their distribution of punishments, that the evil resulting from this cause is not so great and so immediately dangerous to society, as the irregular gratification of the desire of property; but placing this evil in the most formidable point of view we should evidently purchase a diminution of it at a very high price, by the extinction or diminution of the passion which causes it; a change which would probably convert human life either into a cold and cheerless blank or a scene of savage and merciless ferocity.

A careful attention to the remote as well as immediate effect of all the human passions and all the general laws of nature, leads us strongly to the conclusion that under the present constitution of things few or none of them will admit of being greatly diminished, without narrowing the sources of good more powerfully than the sources of evil. And the reason seems to be obvious. They are in fact the materials of all our pleasures as well as of all our pains; of all our happiness as well as of all our misery; of all our virtues as well as of all our vices. It must therefore be regulation and direction that are wanted, not diminution or extinction.

It is justly observed by Paley, that "Human passions are either necessary to human welfare, or capable of being made, and in a great majority of instances are in fact made, conducive to its happiness. These passions are strong and general; and perhaps would not answer their purpose unless they were so. But strength and generality, when it is expedient that particular circumstances should be respected, become if left to themselves excess and misdirection. From which excess and misdirection the vices of mankind (the causes no doubt of much misery) appear to spring. This account, while it shows us the principle of vice, shows us at the same time the province of reason and self-government."[1]

Our virtue therefore as reasonable beings evidently consists in educing from the general materials which the Creator has placed under our guidance the greatest sum of human happiness; and as natural impulses are abstractedly considered good, and only to be distinguished by their consequences, a strict attention to these consequences and the regulation of our conduct conformably to them must be considered as our principal duty.

The fecundity of the human species is in some respects a distinct consideration from the passion between the sexes, as it evidently depends more upon the power of women in bearing children than upon the strength and weakness of this passion. It is a law however exactly similar in its great features to all the other laws of nature. It is strong and general, and apparently would not admit of any very considerable diminution, without being inadequate to its object; the evils arising from it are incidental to those necessary qualities of strength and generality; and these evils are capable of being very greatly mitigated and rendered comparatively light by human energy

---

[1] Natural Theology, c. xlvi. p. 547.

and virtue. We cannot but conceive that it is an object of the Creator that the earth should be replenished; and it appears to me clear that this could not be effected without a tendency in population to increase faster than food; and as, with the present law of increase, the peopling of the earth does not proceed very rapidly, we have undoubtedly some reason to believe that this law is not too powerful for its apparent object. The desire of the means of subsistence would be comparatively confined in its effects, and would fail of producing that general activity so necessary to the improvement of the human faculties, were it not for the strong and universal effort of population to increase with greater rapidity than its supplies. If these two tendencies were exactly balanced, I do not see what motive there would be sufficiently strong to overcome the acknowledged indolence of man, and make him proceed in the cultivation of the soil. The population of any large territory, however fertile, would be as likely to stop at five hundred or five thousand, as at five millions or fifty millions. Such a balance therefore would clearly defeat one great purpose of creation; and if the question be merely a question of degree, a question of a little more or a little less strength, we may fairly distrust our competence to judge of the precise quantity necessary to answer the object with the smallest sum of incidental evil. In the present state of things we appear to have under our guidance a great power, capable of peopling a desert region in a small number of years; and yet under other circumstances capable of being confined by human energy and virtue to any limits, however narrow, at the expense of a small comparative quantity of evil. The analogy of all the other laws of nature would be completely violated, if in this instance alone there were no provision for accidental failures, no resources against the vices of mankind, or the partial mischiefs resulting from other general laws. To effect the apparent object without any attendant evil, it is evident that a perpetual change in the law of increase would be necessary, varying with the varying circumstances of each country. But instead of this it is not only more consonant to the analogy of the other parts of nature, hut we have reason to think that it is more conducive to the formation and improvement of the human mind, that the laws should be uniform and the evils incidental to it, under certain circumstances, left to be mitigated or removed by man himself. His duties in this case vary with his situation; he is thus kept more alive to the consequences of his actions; and his faculties have evidently greater play and opportunity of improvement, than if the evil were removed by a perpetual change of the law according to circumstances.

Even if from passions too easily subdued, or the facility of illicit intercourse, a state of celibacy were a matter of indifference, and not a state of some privation, the end of nature in the peopling of the earth would be apparently liable to be defeated. It is of the very utmost importance to the happiness of mankind that population should not increase too fast; but it does not appear that the object to be accomplished would admit of any considerable diminution in the desire of marriage. It is clearly the duty of each individual not to marry till he has a prospect of supporting his children; but it is at the same time to be wished that he should retain undiminished his desire of marriage, in order that he may exert himself to realise this prospect, and be stimulated to make provision for the support of greater numbers.

It is evidently therefore regulation and direction which are required with regard to the principle of population, not diminution or alteration. And if moral restraint be the only virtuous mode of avoiding the incidental evils arising from this principle, our obligation to practise it will evidently rest exactly upon the same foundation as our obligation to practise any of the other virtues.

Whatever indulgence we may be disposed to allow to occasional failures in the discharge of a duty of acknowledged difficulty, yet of the strict line of duty we cannot doubt. Our obligation not to marry till we have fair prospect of being able to support our children will appear to deserve the attention of the moralist, if it can be proved that an attention to this obligation is of most powerful effect in the prevention of misery: and that if it were the general custom to follow the first impulse of nature and marry at the age of puberty, the universal prevalence of every known virtue in the greatest conceivable degree would fail of rescuing society from the most wretched and desperate state of want, and all the diseases and famines which usually accompany it.

Discussion Questions

1. Summarize Malthus' theory of population. Did his dire predictions of crisis come true? How valid do you think his theories are today? Do natural laws govern the expansion of human beings?

2. How, according to Malthus, can overpopulation and crisis be prevented? Who, or what, is to blame for the increases in population that provoke food shortages?

Sources

Thomas Robert Malthus, *An Essay on the Principle of Population, Or a View of Its Past and Present Effects on Human Happiness*, Seventh Edition [1872], New York: Augustus M. Kelley, 1971.

William Petersen, *Malthus*, Cambridge: Harvard University Press, 1979.

ADAM SMITH,
THE WEALTH OF NATIONS

Adam Smith was born in the port town of Kircaldy, Scotland in 1723. His father, who had been a high-ranking customs agent, died before Smith's birth. At the age of fourteen, Smith was sent to study at the University of Glasgow, where he confronted the great dilemma of how to resolve classical and Christian altruism with more recent arguments that extolled the virtues of self-interest. He then won a scholarship to Oxford. Upon the completion of his studies there, Smith lectured at Edinburgh for a time before he was offered a professorship at the University of Glasgow in 1751, where he taught ethics, jurisprudence, theology, moral philosophy, and the new science of political economy until 1764. He became friends with the philosopher David Hume, and together, they founded the Select Society, a club of lettered men who met to discuss the concerns of the Scottish Enlightenment. Smith then left his post at Glasgow to travel as tutor to the stepson of an English nobleman. He spent time in France, where he made the acquaintance of the Physiocrats, who believed that economics were governed by natural laws.

Smith began to compile *The Wealth of Nations* on the basis of his earlier lectures. The book, published in 1776, established Smith as one of the age's leading liberal thinkers and foremost proponents of laissez-faire economics. He opposed government regulation of the economy, but at the same time, demonstrated considerable sympathy for the plight of working people as the industrial revolution transformed their lives. Shortly after its publication, Smith's intellectual efforts were rewarded by an appointment to Commissioner of Customs, a post he held until the end of his life. He died in 1790, leaving only a modest estate because of the secret charitable contributions he had made in the years preceding his death.

The Wealth of Nations is considered one of the foundational texts of modern economics. Smith presumes that people are driven primarily by self-interest and that people are economic beings. He then argues that by allowing people to strive for their self-interest, society attains the greatest balance. For his critics, Smith sanctioned the predatory practices of the new capitalist class, yet a careful reading reveals his strong sense of social conscience. In the first chapter of *The Wealth of Nations*, excerpted below, Smith explains the division of labor and the remarkable productivity derived from dividing labor among many hands.

THE WEALTH OF NATIONS

Adam Smith

OF THE DIVISION OF LABOUR

The greatest improvement in the productive powers of labour, and the greater part of the skill, dexterity, and judgment with which it is any where directed, or applied, seem to have been the effects of the division of labour.

The effects of the division of labour, in the general business of society, will be more easily understood, by considering in what manner it operates in some particular manufactures. It is commonly supposed to be carried furthest in some very trifling ones; not perhaps that it really is carried further in them than in others of more importance: but in those trifling manufactures which are destined to supply the small wants of but a small number of people, the whole number of workmen must necessarily be small; and those employed in every different branch of the work can often be collected into the same workhouse, and placed at once under the view of the spectator. In those great manufactures, on the contrary, which are destined to supply the great wants of the great body of the people, every different branch of the work employs so great a number of workmen, that it is impossible to collect them all into the same workhouse. We can seldom see more, at one time, than those employed in one single branch. Though in such manufactures, therefore, the work may really be divided into a much greater number of parts, than in those of a more trifling nature, the division is not near so obvious, and has accordingly been much less observed.

To take an example, therefore, from a very trifling manufacture; but one in which the division of labour has been very often taken notice of, the trade of the pin-maker; a workman not educated to this business (which the division of labour has rendered a distinct trade, nor acquainted with the use of the machinery employed in it (to the invention of which the same division of labour has probably given occasion), could scarce, perhaps, with his utmost industry, make one pin in a day, and certainly could not make twenty. But in the way in which this business is now carried on, not only the whole work is a peculiar trade, but it is divided into a number of branches, of which the greater part are likewise peculiar trades. One man draws out the wire, another straights it, a third cuts it, a fourth points it, a fifth grinds it at the top for receiving the head; to make the head requires two or three distinct operations; to put it on, is a peculiar business, to whiten the pins is another; it is even a trade by itself to put them into the paper; and the important business of making a pin is, in this manner, divided into about eighteen distinct operations, which, in some manufactories, are all performed by distinct hands, though in others the same man will sometimes perform two or three of them. I have seen a small manufactory of this kind where ten men only were employed, and where some of them consequently performed two or three distinct operations. But though they were very poor, and therefore but indifferently accommodated with the necessary machinery, they could, when they exerted themselves, make among them about twelve pounds of pins in a day. There are in a pound upwards of four thousand pins of a middling size. Those ten persons, therefore, could make among them upwards of forty-eight thousand pins in a day. Each person, therefore, making a tenth part of forty-eight thousand pins, might be considered as making four thousand eight hundred pins in a day. But if they had all wrought separately and independently, and without any of them having been educated to this peculiar business, they certainly could not each of them have made twenty, perhaps not one pin in a day; that is, certainly, not the two hundred and fortieth, perhaps not the four thousand eight hundredth part of what they are at present capable of performing, in consequence of a proper division and combination of their different operations.

In every other art and manufacture, the effects of the division of labour are similar to what they are in this very trifling one; though, in many of them, the labour can neither be so much subdivided, nor reduced to so great a simplicity of operation. The division of labour, however, so far as it can be introduced, occasions, in every art, a proportionable increase of the productive powers of labour. The separation of different trades and employments from one another, seems to have taken place, in consequence of this advantage. This separation too is generally carried furthest in those countries which enjoy the highest degree of industry and improvement; what is the work of one man in a rude state of society, being generally that of several in an improved one. In every improved society, the farmer is generally nothing but a farmer; the manufacturer, nothing but a manufacturer. The labour too which is necessary to produce any one complete manufacture, is almost always divided among a great number of hands. How many different trades are employed in each branch of the linen and woollen manufactures, from the growers of the flax and the wool, to the bleachers and smoothers of the linen, or to the dyers and dressers of the cloth! The nature of agriculture, indeed, does not admit of so many subdivisions of labour, nor of so complete a separation of one business from another, as manufactures. It is impossible to separate so entirely, the business of the grazier from that of the corn-farmer, as the trade of the carpenter is commonly separated from that of the smith. The spinner is almost always a distinct person from the weaver; but the ploughman, the harrower, the sower of the seed, and the reaper of the corn, are often the same. The occasions for those different sorts of labour returning with the different seasons of the year, it is impossible that one man should be constantly employed in any one of them. This impossibility of making so complete and entire a separation of all the different branches of labour employed in agriculture, is perhaps the reason why the improvement of the productive powers of labour in this art, does not always keep pace with their improvement in manufactures. The most opulent nations, indeed, generally excel all their neighbours in agriculture as well as in manufactures; but they are commonly more distinguished by their superiority in the latter than in the former. Their lands are in general better cultivated, and having more labour and expence bestowed upon them, produce more in proportion to the extent and natural fertility of the ground. But this superiority of produce is seldom much more than in proportion to the superiority of labour and expence. In agriculture, the labour of the rich country is not always much more productive than that of the poor; or, at least, it is never so much more productive, as it commonly is in manufactures. The corn of the rich country, therefore, will not always, in the same degree of goodness, come cheaper to market than that of the poor. The corn of Poland, in the same degree of goodness, is as cheap as that of France, notwithstanding the superior opulence and improvement of the latter country. The corn of France is, in the corn provinces, fully as good, and in most years nearly about the same price with the corn of England, though, in opulence and improvement, France is perhaps inferior to England. The corn-lands of England, however, are better cultivated than those of France, and the corn-lands of France are said to be much better cultivated than those of Poland. But though the poor country, notwithstanding the inferiority of its cultivation, can, in some measure, rival the rich in the cheapness and goodness of its corn, it can pretend to no such competition in its manufactures; at least if those manufactures suit the soil, climate, and situation of the rich country. The silks of France are better and cheaper than those of England, because the silk manufacture, at least under the present high duties upon the importation of raw silk, does not so well suit the climate of England as that of France. But the hard-ware and the coarse woollens of England are beyond all comparison superior to those of France, and much cheaper too in the same degree of goodness. In Poland there are said to be scarce any manufactures of any kind, a few of those coarser household manufactures excepted, without which no country can well subsist.

This great increase of the quantity of work, which, in consequence of the division of labour, the same number of people are capable of performing, is owing to three different circumstances; first, to the increase of dexterity in every particular workman; secondly, to the saving of the time which is commonly lost in passing from one species of work to another; and lastly, to the invention of a great number of machines which facilitate and abridge labour, and enable one man to do the work of many.

First, the improvement of the dexterity of the workman necessarily increases the quantity of the work he can perform; and the division of labour, by reducing every man's business to some one simple operation, and by making this operation the sole employment of his life, necessarily increases very much the dexterity of the workman. A common smith, who, though accustomed to handle the hammer, has never been used to make nails, if upon some particular occasion he is obliged to attempt it, will scarce, I am assured, be able to make above two or three hundred nails in a day, and those too very bad ones. A smith who has been accustomed to make nails, but whose sole or principal business has not been that of a nailer, can seldom with his utmost diligence make more than eight hundred or a thousand nails in a day. I have seen several boys under twenty years of age who had never exercised any other trade but that of making nails, and who, when they exerted themselves, could make, each of them, upwards of two thousand three hundred nails in a day. The making of a nail, however, is by no means one of the simplest operations. The same person blows the bellows, stirs or mends the fire as there is occasion, heats the iron, and forges every part of the nail: In forging the head too he is obliged to change his tools. The different operations into which the making of a pin, or of a metal button, is subdivided, are all of them much more simple, and the dexterity of the person, of whose life it has been the sole business to perform them, is usually much greater. The rapidity with which some of the operations of those manufactures are performed, exceeds what the human hand could, by those who had never seen them, be supposed capable of acquiring.

Secondly, the advantage which is gained by saving the time commonly lost in passing from one sort of work to another, is much greater than we should at first view be apt to imagine it. It is impossible to pass very quickly from one kind of work to another, that is carried on in a different place, and with quite different tools. A country weaver, who cultivates a small farm, must lose a good deal of time in passing from his loom to the field, and from the field to his loom. When the two trades can be carried on in the same workhouse, the loss of time is no doubt much less. It is even in this case, however, very considerable. A man commonly saunters a little in turning his hand from one sort of employment to another. When he first begins the new work he is seldom very keen and hearty; his mind, as they say, does not go to it, and for some time he rather trifles than applies to good purpose. The habit of sauntering and of indolent careless application, which is naturally, or rather necessarily acquired by every country workman who is obliged to change his work and his tools every half hour, and to apply his hand in twenty different ways almost every day of his life; renders him almost always slothful and lazy, and incapable of any vigorous application even on the most pressing occasions. Independent, therefore, of his deficiency in point of dexterity, this cause alone must always reduce considerably the quantity of work which he is capable of performing.

Thirdly, and lastly, every body must be sensible how much labour is facilitated and abridged by the, application of proper machinery. It is unnecessary to give any example. I shall only observe, therefore, that the invention of all those machines by which labour is so much facilitated and abridged, seems to have been originally owing to the division of labour. Men are much more likely to discover easier and readier methods of attaining any object, when the whole attention of their minds is directed towards that single object, than when it is dissipated among a great variety of things. But in consequence of the division of labour, the whole of every man's attention comes naturally to be directed towards some one very simple object. It is naturally to be expected, therefore, that some one or other of those who are employed in each particular branch of labour should soon find out easier and readier methods of performing their own particular work, wherever the nature of it admits of such improvement. A great part of the machines made use of in those manufactures in which labour is most subdivided, were originally the inventions of common workmen, who, being each of them employed in some very simple operation, naturally turned their thoughts towards finding out easier and readier methods of performing it. Whoever has been much accustomed to visit such manufactures, must frequently have been shewn very pretty machines, which were the inventions of such workmen, in order to facilitate and quicken their own particular part of the work. In the first fire-engines, a boy was constantly employed to open and shut alternately the communication between the boiler and the cylinder, according as the piston either ascended or descended. One of those boys, who loved to play with his companions, observed that, by tying a string from the handle of the valve which opened this communication to another part of the machine, the valve would open and shut without his assistance, and leave him at liberty to divert himself with his play-fellows. One of the greatest improvements that has been made upon this machine, since it was first invented, was in this manner the discovery of a boy who wanted to save his own labour.

All the improvements in machinery, however, have by no means been the inventions of those who has occasion to use the machines. Many improvements have been made by the ingenuity of the makers of the machines, when to make them became the business of a peculiar trade; and some by that of those who are called philosophers or men of speculation, whose trade it is not to do any thing, but to observe every thing; and who, upon that account, are often capable of combining together the powers of the most distant and dissimilar objects. In the progress of society, philosophy or speculation becomes, like every other employment, the principal or sole trade and occupation of a particular class of citizens. Like every other employment too, it is subdivided into a great number of different branches, each of which affords occupation to a peculiar tribe or class of philosophers; and this subdivision of employment in philosophy, as well as in every other business, improves dexterity, and saves time. Each individual becomes more expert in his own peculiar branch, more work is done upon the whole, and the quantity of science is considerably increased by it.

It is the great multiplication of the productions of all the different arts, in consequence of the division of labour, which occasions, in a well-governed society, that universal opulence which extends itself to the lowest ranks of the people. Every workman has a great quantity of his own work to dispose of beyond what he himself has occasion for; and every other workman being exactly in the same situation, he is enabled to exchange a great quantity of his own goods for a great quantity, or, what comes to the same thing, for the price of a great quantity of theirs. He supplies them abundantly with what they have occasion for, and they accommodate him as amply with what he has occasion for, and a general plenty diffuses itself through all the different ranks of the society.

Observe the accommodation of the most common artificer or day-labourer in a civilized and thriving country, and you will perceive that the number of people of whose industry a part, though but a small part, has been employed in procuring him this accommodation, exceeds all computation. The woollen coat, for example, which covers the day-labourer, as coarse and rough as it may appear, is the produce of the joint labour of a great multitude of workmen. The shepherd, the sorter of the wool, the wool-comber or carder, the dyer, the scribbler, the spinner, the weaver, the fuller, the dresser, with many others, must all join their different arts in order to complete even this homely production. How many merchants and carriers, besides, must have been employed in transporting the materials from some of those workmen to others who often live in a very distant part of the country! how much commerce and navigation in particular, how many shipbuilders, sailors, sail-makers, rope-makers, must have been employed in order to bring together the different drugs made use of by the dyer, which often come from the remotest corners of the world! What a variety of labour too is necessary in order to produce the tools of the meanest of those workmen! To say nothing of such complicated machines as the ship of the sailor, the mill of the fuller, or even the loom of the weaver, let us consider only what a variety of labour is requisite in order to form that very simple machine, the shears with which the shepherd clips the wool. The miner, the builder of the furnace for smelting the ore, the feller of the timber, the burner of the charcoal to be made use of in the smelting-house, the brick-maker, the brick-layer, the workmen who attend the furnace, the mill-wright, the forger, the smith, must all of them join their different arts in order to produce them. Were we to examine, in the same manner, all the different parts of his dress and household furniture, the coarse linen shirt which he wears next his skin, the shoes which cover his feet, the bed which he lies on, and all the different parts which compose it, the kitchen-grate at which he prepares his victuals, the coals which he makes use of for that purpose, dug from the bowels of the earth, and brought to him perhaps by a long sea and a long land carriage, all the other utensils of his kitchen, all the furniture of his table, the knives and forks, the earthen or pewter plates upon which he serves up and divides his victuals, the different hands employed in preparing his bread and, his beer, the glass window which lets in the heat and the light, and keeps out the wind and the rain, with all the knowledge and art requisite for preparing that beautiful and happy invention, without which these northern parts of the world could scarce have afforded a very comfortable habitation, together with the tools of all the different workmen employed in producing those different conveniencies; if we examine, I say, all these things, and consider what a variety of labour is employed about each of them, we shall be sensible that without the assistance and co-operation of many thousands, the very meanest person in a civilized country could not be provided, even according to, what we very falsely imagine, the easy and simple manner in which he is commonly accommodated. Compared, indeed, with the more extravagant luxury of the great, his accommodation must no doubt appear extremely simple and easy; and yet it may be true, perhaps, that the accommodation of an European prince does not always so much exceed that of an industrious and frugal peasant, as the accommodation of the latter exceeds that of many an African king, the absolute master of the lives and liberties of ten thousand naked savages.

Discussion Questions

1. Why, or how, according to Smith, does the division of labor increase productivity?
2. What are the benefits of the division of labor for individuals? For societies?

Sources

Adam Smith, *An Inquiry into the Nature and Causes of the Wealth of Nations*, New York: Random House, 1937.

Jerry Z. Muller, *Adam Smith in His Times and Ours: Designing the Decent Society*, New York: The Free Press, 1993.

CHAPTER 18

Karl Marx and Friedrich Engels
The Communist Manifesto

George Eliot
Felix Holt

KARL MARX AND FRIEDRICH ENGELS, *THE COMMUNIST MANIFESTO*

Karl Marx, the primary author of *The Communist Manifesto*, was as much a product of the Enlightenment as he was one of its leading critics. Born a Jew in 1818 in Trier, then part of Prussia, Marx demonstrated little radicalism until his years at the University of Berlin. He had begun to study law at the University of Bonn in 1835, but transferred to Berlin a year later. There, he joined the Young Hegelians, who questioned the rationality and empirical emphases of the Enlightenment, by way of challenging the conservative climate of Germany. They advanced the idea that all history was struggle, a concept that Marx would appropriate for his critiques of capitalism and progress. Marx threw himself into the study of Hegel at the expense of his law career, and soon devoted himself to philosophy. He also became secretly engaged to Jenny Westphalen, whom he married in 1843, very much against the wishes of her family. The young couple emigrated to Paris, where Marx became more radicalized by his contact with workers.

In 1844, while still in Paris, Marx met Engels, the son of an English industrialist. Their friendship and collaboration endured until Marx's death. Engels rescued the Marx family from the brink of poverty on more than one occasion. In 1845, Marx was expelled from Paris in 1845 at the demand of the Prussian government. The Marx family first fled to Brussels, where he made contact with German workers, whose ultimate goal was to create an international workers organization. They finally journeyed to London, where they remained until Marx's death in 1883. Marx, who never became a public personality or charismatic political leader during his time, spent the latter half of his life writing and theorizing about history, capitalism, and exploitation.

In 1847 the London chapter of the Communist League, then a German organization, later international, commissioned a document outlining their vision of revolutionary change. Marx and Engels labored over this document together, producing one of the most enduring calls to revolutionary action ever written. *The Communist Manifesto* was published just before the working classes were sorely defeated in the revolutions of 1848. According to Engels, Marx deserves credit for the main thesis of the *Manifesto*. Marx proposed that all history had revolved around class struggle. Only by defeating their oppressors could the oppressed classes attain emancipation. In the passage below, Marx describes the successes of the bourgeoisie in overcoming feudalism, and begins to outline the challenges facing them from the proletariat.

THE COMMUNIST MANIFESTO

Karl Marx and Friedrich Engels

The history of all hitherto existing society is the history of class struggles.

Freeman and slave, patrician and plebeian, lord and serf, guild-master and journeyman, in a word, oppressor and oppressed, stood in constant opposition to one another, carried on an uninterrupted, now hidden, now open fight, a fight that each rime ended, either in a revolutionary reconstitution of society at large, or in the common ruin of the contending classes.

In the earlier epochs of history, we find almost everywhere a complicated arrangement of society into various orders, a manifold gradation of social rank. In ancient Rome we have patricians, knights, plebelans, slaves; in the Middle Ages, feudal lords, vassals, guild-masters, journeymen, apprentices, serfs; in almost all of these classes, again, subordinate gradations.

The modern bourgeois society that has sprouted from the ruins of feudal society, has not done away with class antagonisms. It has but established new classes, new conditions of oppression, new forms of struggle in place of the old ones.

Our epoch, the epoch of the bourgeoisie, possesses, however, this distinctive feature: It has simplified the class antagonisms. Society as a whole is more and more splitting up into two great hostile camps, into two great classes directly facing each other—bourgeoisie and proletariat.

From the serfs of the Middle Ages sprang the chartered burghers of the earliest towns. From these burgesses the first elements of the bourgeoisie were developed.

The discovery of America, the rounding of the Cape, opened up fresh ground for the rising bourgeoisie. The East Indian and Chinese markets, the colonization of America, trade with the colonies, the increase in the means of exchange and in commodities generally, gave to commerce, to navigation, to industry, an impulse never before known, and thereby, to the revolutionary element in the tottering feudal society, a rapid development.

The feudal system of industry, in which industrial production was monopolized by closed guilds, now no longer sufficed for the growing wants of the new markets. The manufacturing system took its place. The guild-masters were pushed aside by the manufacturing middle class; division of labor between the different corporate guilds vanished in the face of division of labor in each single workshop.

Meantime the markets kept ever growing, the demand ever rising. Even manufacture no longer sufficed. Thereupon, steam and machinery revolutionized industrial production. The place of manufacture was taken by the giant, modern industry, the place of the industrial middle class, by industrial millionaires-the leaders of whole industrial armies, the modern bourgeois.

Modern industry has established the world market, for which the discovery of America paved the way. This market has given an immense development to commerce, to navigation, to communication by land. This development has, in its turn, reacted on the extension of industry; and in proportion as industry, commerce, navigation, railways extended, in the same proportion the bourgeoisie developed, increased its capital, and pushed into the background every class handed down from the Middle Ages.

We see, therefore, how the modern bourgeoisie is itself the product of a long course of development, of a series of revolutions in the modes of production and of exchange.

Each step in the development of the bourgeoisie was accompanied by a corresponding political advance of that class. An oppressed class under the sway of the feudal nobility, it became an armed and self-governing association in the medieval commune; here independent urban republic (as in Italy and Germany), there taxable "third estate" of the monarchy (as in France); afterwards, in the period of manufacture proper, serving either the semi-feudal or the absolute monarchy as a counterpoise against the nobility, and, in fact, cornerstone of the great monarchies in general—the bourgeoisie has at last, since the establishment of modern industry and of the world market, conquered for itself, in the modern representative state, exclusive political sway. The executive of the modern state is but a committee for managing the common affairs of the whole bourgeoisie.

The bourgeoisie has played a most revolutionary role in history.

The bourgeoisie, wherever it has got the upper hand, has put an end to all feudal, patriarchal, idyllic relations. It has pitilessly torn asunder the motley feudal ties that bound man to his "natural superiors," and has left no other bond between man and man than naked self-interest, than callous "cash payment." It has drowned the most heavenly ecstasies of religious fervor, of chivalrous enthusiasm, of philistine sentimentalism, in the icy water of egotistical calculation. It has resolved personal worth into exchange value, and in place of the numberless indefeasible chartered freedoms, has set up that single, unconscionable freedom—Free Trade. In one word, for exploitation, veiled by religious and political illusions, it has substituted naked, shameless, direct, brutal exploitation.

The bourgeoisie has stripped of its halo every occupation hitherto honored and looked up to with reverent awe. It has converted the physician, the lawyer, the priest, the poet, the man of science, into its paid wage-laborers.

The bourgeoisie has torn away from the family its sentimental veil, and has reduced the family relation to a mere money relation.

The bourgeoisie has disclosed how it came to pass that the brutal display of vigor in the Middle Ages, which reactionaries so much admire, found its fitting complement in the most slothful indolence. It has been the first to show what man's activity can bring about. It has accomplished wonders far surpassing Egyptian pyramids, Roman aqueducts, and Gothic cathedrals; it has conducted expeditions that put in the shade all former migrations of nations and crusades.

The bourgeoisie cannot exist without constantly revolutionizing the instruments of production, and thereby the relations of production, and with them the whole relations of society. Conservation of the old modes of production in unaltered form, was, on the contrary, the first condition of existence for all earlier industrial classes. Constant revolutionizing of production, uninterrupted disturbance of all social conditions, everlasting uncertainty and agitation distinguish the bourgeois epoch from all earlier ones. All fixed, fast-frozen relations, with their train of ancient and venerable prejudices and opinions, are swept away, all new-formed ones become antiquated before they can ossify. All that is solid melts into air, all that is holy is profaned, and man is at last compelled to face with sober senses his real conditions of life and his relations with his kind.

The need of a constantly expanding market for its products chases the bourgeoisie over the whole surface of the globe. It must nestle everywhere, settle everywhere, establish connections everywhere.

The bourgeoisie has through its exploitation of the world market given a cosmopolitan character to production and consumption in every country. To the great chagrin of reactionaries, it has drawn from under the feet of industry the national ground on which it stood. All old-established national industries have been destroyed or are daily being destroyed. They are dislodged by new industries, whose introduction becomes a life and death question for all civilized nations, by industries that no longer work up indigenous raw material, but raw material drawn from the remotest zones; industries whose products are consumed, not only at home, but in every quarter of the globe. In place of the old wants, satisfied by the production of the country, we find new wants, requiring for their satisfaction the products of distant lands and climes. In place of the old local and national seclusion and self-sufficiency, we have intercourse in every direction, universal inter-dependence of nations. And as in material, so also in intellectual production. The intellectual creations of individual nations become common property. National one-sidedness and narrow-mindedness become more and more impossible, and from the numerous national and local literatures there arises a world literature.

The bourgeoisie, by the rapid improvement of all instruments of production, by the immensely facilitated means of communication, draws all nations, even the most barbarian, into civilization. The cheap prices of its commodities are the heavy artillery with which it batters down all Chinese walls, with which it forces the barbarians' intensely obstinate hatred of foreigners to capitulate. It compels all nations, on pain of extinction, to adopt the bourgeois mode of production; it compels them to introduce what it calls civilization into their midst, i.e., to become bourgeois themselves. In a word, it creates a world after its own image.

The bourgeoisie has subjected the country to the rule of the towns. It has created enormous cities, has greatly increased the urban population as compared with the rural, and has thus rescued a considerable part of the population from the idiocy of rural life. Just as it has made the country dependent on the towns, so it has made barbarian and semi-barbarian countries dependent on the civilized ones, nations of peasants on nations of bourgeois, the East on the West.

More and more the bourgeoisie keeps doing away with the scattered state of the population, of the means of production, and of property. It has agglomerated population, centralized means of production, and has concentrated property in a few hands. The necessary consequence of this was political centralization. Independent, or but loosely connected provinces, with separate interests, laws, governments, and systems of taxation, became lumped together into one nation, with one government, one code of laws, one national class interest, one frontier, and one customs tariff.

The bourgeoisie, during its rule of scarce one hundred years has created more massive and more colossal productive forces than have all preceding generations together. Subjection of nature's forces to man, machinery, application of chemistry to industry and agriculture, steam-navigation, railways, electric telegraphs, clearing of whole continents for cultivation, canalisation of rivers, whole populations conjured out of the ground—what earlier century had even a presentiment that such productive forces slumbered in the lap of social labour?

We see then that the means of production and of exchange, which served as the foundation for the growth of the bourgeoisie, were generated in feudal society. At a certain stage in the development of these means of production and of exchange, the conditions under which feudal society produced and exchanged, the feudal organisation of agriculture and manufacturing industry, in a word, the feudal relations of property became no longer compatible with the already developed productive forces; they became so many fetters. They had to be burst asunder; they were burst asunder.

Into their place stepped free competition, accompanied by a social and political constitution adapted to it, and by the economic and political sway of the bourgeois class.

A similar movement is going on before our own eyes. Modern bourgeois society with its relations of production, of exchange and of property, a society that has conjured up such gigantic means of production and of exchange, is like the sorcerer who is no longer able to control the powers of the nether world whom he has called up by his spells. For many a decade past the history of industry and commerce is but the history of the revolt of modern productive forces against modern conditions of production, against the property relations that are the conditions for the existence of the bourgeoisie and of its rule. It is enough to mention the commercial crises that by their periodical return put the existence of the entire bourgeois society on trial, each time more threateningly. In these crises a great part not only of the existing products, but also of the previously created productive forces, are periodically destroyed. In these crises there breaks out an epidemic that, in all earlier epochs, would have seemed an absurdity— the epidemic of over-production. Society suddenly finds itself put back into a state of momentary barbarism; it appears as if a famine, a universal war of devastation had cut off the supply of every means of subsistence; industry and commerce seem to be destroyed. And why? Because there is too much civilization, too much means of subsistence, too much industry, too much commerce. The productive forces at the disposal of society no longer tend to further the development of the conditions of bourgeois property; on the contrary, they have become too powerful for these conditions, by which they are fettered, and no sooner do they overcome these fetters than they bring disorder into the whole of bourgeois society, endanger the existence of bourgeois property. The conditions of bourgeois society are too narrow to comprise the wealth created by them. And how does the bourgeoisie get over these crises? On the one hand, by enforced destruction of a mass of productive forces; on the other, by the conquest of new markets, and by the more thorough exploitation of the old ones. That is to say, by paving the way for more extensive and more destructive crises, and by diminishing the means whereby crises are prevented.

Discussion Questions

1. How do Marx and Engels portray the bourgeoisie?
2. How critical are Marx and Engels of capitalism and progress?

Sources

Karl Marx and Frederick Engels, *Manifesto of the Communist Party*, New York: International Publishers, 1948.

Isaiah Berlin, *Karl Marx: His Life and Environment*, New York and Oxford: Oxford University Press, 1996.

GEORGE ELIOT,
FELIX HOLT

George Eliot was born Mary Anne Evans in 1819 in Warwickshire, England. She was educated at Miss Lathom's school in Attleborough until 1828, when she transferred to Miss Wallington's school in Nuneaton. In her studies, she concentrated on Latin and French. When her mother died in 1836, Eliot returned home to accompany her father in his retirement. She grew close to her neighbors Charles and Caroline Bray and their family, who provided Eliot with a new intellectual stimulation. Her father's death in 1849 permitted Eliot to work as a translator and to travel for a few years on the small inheritance that he had left her.

In 1850, the Westminster Review offered Eliot an editorship, which brought her into contact with the many of the period's foremost intellectuals. Her acquaintance with the writer and philosopher George Henry Lewes led to a lasting love affair. Lewes, unable to divorce his wife, lived with Eliot until his death in 1878. After a lengthy tour of Europe in the company of her newfound companion, Eliot began to publish articles. She also experimented with fiction. She adopted the name George Eliot in the late 1850s as her writing career gained momentum. Her first novels, *Adam Bede*, *The Mill on the Floss*, and *Silas Marner*, earned her the critical praise of contemporaries like Charles Dickens and William Makepeace Thackeray. She had attained both commercial success and literary excellence as a novelist, a rare achievement in any period.

Felix Holt, Eliot's first explicitly political novel, was written in 1865 and 1866 over the course of fourteen months. Set just after 1832 in a Midlands town undergoing a dramatic transformation due to the advent of the industrial revolution, the novel is narrated through the eyes of Felix Holt, a Radical and Positivist from working class origins. Eliot's portrayal of the politics surrounding the passing of the Reform Bill and the troubles of working people as the industrial revolution accelerated revealed her meticulous style. The passage of the Reform Bill in 1832 meant significant steps toward democratizing the vote in nineteenth century England. It increased the franchise and attempted to curb some of the more blatant instances of electoral corruption. However, the main character of the novel, Felix, remained skeptical. In the scene below, Felix has traveled to Duffield to see the North Loamshire candidates nominated. The polls had closed, and Felix paused on a street corner to listen to a speaker, who was attacking the superficiality of the Reform Bill, advocating a deeper reform that included universal suffrage. Felix speaks up in agreement at first, but then argues that the pursuit of the vote would ultimately prove futile.

FELIX HOLT

George Eliot

The group round the speaker in the flannel shirt stood at the corner of a side street, and the speaker himself was elevated by the head and shoulders above his hearers, not because he was tall, but because he stood on a projecting stone. At the opposite corner of the turning was the great inn of the Fox and Hounds, and this was the ultra-Liberal quarter of the High Street. Felix was at once attracted by this group; he liked the look of the speaker, whose bare arms were powerfully muscular, though he had the pallid complexion of a man who lives chiefly amidst the heat of furnaces. He was leaning against the dark atone building behind him with folded arms, the grimy paleness of his shirt and skin standing out in high relief against the dark stone building behind him. He lifted up one fore finger, and marked his emphasis with it as he spoke. His voice was high and not strong, but Felix recognized the fluency and the method of a habitual preacher or lecturer.

"It's the fallacy of all monopolists," he was saying. "We know what monopolists are: men who want to keep a trade all to themselves, under the pretence that they'll furnish the public with a better article. We know what that comes to: in some countries a poor man can't afford to buy a spoonful of salt, and yet there's salt enough in the world to pickle every living thing in it. That's the sort of benefit monopolists do to mankind. And these are the men who tell us we're to let politics alone; they'll govern us better without our knowing anything about it. We must mind our business; we are ignorant; we've no time to study great questions. But I tell them this: the greatest question in the world is, how to give every man a man's share in what goes on in life----"

"Hear, hear!" said Felix in his sonorous voice, which seemed to give a new impressiveness to what the speaker had said. Every one looked at him: the well-washed face and its educated expression, along with a dress more careless than that of most well-to-do workmen on a holiday, made his appearance strangely arresting.

"Not a pig's share," the speaker went on, "not a horse's share, not the share of a machine fed with oil only to make it work and nothing else. It isn't a man's share just to mind your pin-making, or your glass-blowing, and higgle about your own wages, and bring up your family to be ignorant sons of ignorant fathers, and no better prospect; that's a slave's share; we want a freeman's share, and that is to think and speak and act about what concerns us all, and see whether these fine gentlemen who undertake to govern us are doing the best they can for us. They've got the knowledge, say they. Very well, we've got the wants. There's many a one would be idle if hunger didn't pinch him; but the stomach sets us to work. There's a fable told where the nobles are the belly and the people the members. But I make another sort of fable. I say, we are the belly that feels the pinches, and we'll set these aristocrats, these great people who call themselves our brains, to work at some way of satisfying us a bit better. The aristocrats are pretty sure to try and govern for their own benefit; but how are we to be sure they'll try and govern for ours? They must be looked after, I think, like other workmen. We must have what we call inspectors, to see whether the work's well done for us. We want to send our inspectors to Parliament. Well, they say—you've got the Reform Bill; what more can you want? Send your inspectors. But I say, the Reform Bill is a trick—it's nothing but swearing in special constables to keep the aristocrats safe in their monopoly; it's bribing some of the people with votes to make them hold their tongues about giving votes to the rest. I say, if a man doesn't beg or steal, but works for his bread, the poorer and the more miserable he is, the more he'd need have a vote to send an inspector to Parliament—else the man who is worst off is likely to be forgotten; and I say, he's the man who ought to be first remembered. Else what does their religion mean? Why do they build churches and endow them that their sons may get paid well for preaching a Saviour, and making themselves as little like Him as can be? If I want to believe in Jesus Christ, I must shut my eyes for fear I should see a parson. And what's a bishop? A bishop's a parson dressed up, who sits in the House of Lords to help and throw out Reform Bills. And because it's hard to get anything in the shape of a man to dress himself up like that, and do such work, they give him a palace for it, and plenty of thousands a year. And then they cry out—'The Church is in danger,'—'the poor man's Church.' And why is it the poor man's Church? Because he can have a seat for nothing. I think it *is* for nothing; for it would be hard to tell what he gets by it. If the poor man had a vote in the matter, I think he'd choose a different sort of a Church to what that is. But do you think the aristocrats will ever alter it if the belly doesn't pinch them? Not they. It's part of their monopoly. They'll supply us with our religion like everything else, and get a profit on it. They'll give us plenty of heaven. We may have land *there*. That's the sort of religion they like—a religion that gives us working men heaven, and nothing else. But we'll offer to change with 'em. We'll give them back some of their heaven, and take it out in something for us and our children in this world. They don't seem to care so much about heaven themselves till they feel the gout very bad; but you won't get them to give up anything else if you don't pinch 'em for it. And to pinch them enough, we must get the suffrage, we must get votes, that we may send the men to Parliament who will do our work for us; and we must have Parliament dissolved every year, that we may change our man if he doesn't do what we want him to do; and we must have the country divided so that the little kings of the counties can't do as they like, but must be shaken up in one bag with us. I say, if we working men are ever to get a man's share, we must have universal suffrage, and annual Parliaments, and the vote by ballot, and electoral districts."

"No!—something else before all that," said Felix, again startling the audience into looking at him. But the speaker glanced coldly at him and went on.

"That's what Sir Francis Burdett went in for fifteen years, ago; and it's the right thing for us, if it was Tomfool who went in for it. You must lay hold of such handles as you can. I don't believe much in liberal aristocrats; but if there's any fine carved gold-headed stick of an aristocrat will make a broomstick of himself, I'll lose no time but I'll sweep with him. And that's what I think about Transome. And if any of you have acquaintance among county voters, give 'em a hint that you wish 'em to vote for Transome."

At the last word, the speaker stepped down from his slight eminence, and walked away rapidly, like a man whose leisure was exhausted, and who must go about his business. But he had left an appetite in his audience for further oratory, and of them seemed to express a general sentiment as he turned immediately to Felix, and said: "Come, sir, what do you say?"

Felix did at once what he would very likely have done out being asked—he stepped on to the stone, and took off cap by an instinctive prompting that always led him to speak uncovered. The effect of his figure in relief against the stone background was unlike that of the previous speaker. He was considerably taller, his head and neck were more massive, and the expression of his mouth and eyes was something very different from the mere acuteness and rather hard-lipped antagonism of the trades-union man. Felix Holt's face had the look of habitual meditative abstraction from objects of mere personal vanity or desire which is the peculiar stamp of culture, and makes a very roughly cut face worthy to be called "the human face divine." Even lions and dogs know a distinction between men's glances; and doubtless those Duffield men, in the expectation with which they looked up at Felix, were unconsciously influenced by the grandeur of his full yet firm mouth, and the calm clearness of his gray eyes, which were somehow unlike what they were accustomed to see along with an old brown velveteen coat and an absence of chin-propping. When he began to speak, the contrast of voice was still stronger than that of appearance. The man in the flannel shirt had not been heard—had probably not cared to be heard—beyond the immediate group of listeners. But Felix at once drew the attention of persons comparatively at a distance.

"In my opinion," he said, almost the moment after he was addressed, "that was a true word spoken by your friend when he said the great question was how to give every man a man's share in life. But I think he expects voting to do more toward it than I do. I want the working men to have power. I'm a working man myself, and I don't want to be anything else. But there are two sorts of power. There's a power to do mischief—to undo what has been done with great expense and labor, to waste and destroy, to be cruel to the weak, to lie and quarrel, and to talk poisonous nonsense. That's the sort of power that ignorant numbers have. It never made a joint stool or planted a potato. Do you think it's likely to do much toward governing a great country, and making wise laws, and giving shelter, food, and clothes to millions of men? Ignorant power corner in the end to the same thing as wicked power; it makes misery. It's another sort of power that I want us working men to have, and I can see plainly enough that our all having votes will do little toward it at present. I hope we, or the children that come after us, will get plenty of political power some time. I tell everybody plainly, I hope there will be great changes, and that some time, whether we live to see it or not, men will have come to be ashamed of things they're proud of now. But I should like to convince you that votes would never give you political power worth having while things are as they are now, and that if you go the right way to work you may get power sooner without votes. Perhaps all you who hear me are sober men, who try to learn as much of the nature of things as you can, and to be as little like fools as possible. A fool or idiot is one who expects things to happen that never can happen; he pours milk into a can without a bottom, and expects the milk to stay there. The more of such vain expectations a man has, the more he is of a fool or idiot. And if any working man expects a vote to do for him what it never can. do, he's foolish to that amount, if no more. I think that's clear enough, eh?"

"Hear, hear," said several voices, but they were not those of the original group; they belonged to some strollers who had been attracted by Felix Holt' s vibrating voice, and were Tories from the Crown. Among them was Christian, who was smoking a cigar with a pleasure he always felt in being among people who did not know him, and doubtless took him to be something higher than he really was. Hearers from the Fox and Hounds also were slowly adding themselves to the nucleus. Felix, accessible to the pleasure of being listened to, went on with more and more animation:—

"The way to get rid of folly is to get rid of vain expectations, and of thoughts that don't agree with the nature of things. The men who have had true thoughts about water, and what it will do when it is turned into steam and under all sorts of circumstances, have made themselves a great power in the world: they are turning the wheels of engines that will help to change most things. But no engines would have done if there had been false notions about the way water would act. Now, all the schemes about voting, and districts, and annual Parliaments, and the rest, are engines, and the water or steam—the force that is to work them—must come out of human nature—out of men's passions, feelings, desires. Whether the engines will do good work or bad depends on these feelings; and if we have false expectations about men's characters, we are very much like the idiot who thinks he'll carry milk in a can without a bottom. In my opinion, the notions about what mere voting will do are very much of that sort."

"That's very fine," said a man in dirty fustian, with a scornful laugh. "But how are we to get the power without votes?"

"I'll tell you what's the greatest power under heaven," said Felix, "and that is public opinion—the ruling belief in society about what is right and what is wrong, what is honorable and what is shameful. That's the steam that is to work the engines. How can political freedom make us better, any more than a religion we don't believe in, if people laugh and wink when they see men abuse and defile it? And while public opinion is what it is—while men have no better beliefs about public duty—while corruption is not felt to be a damning disgrace while men are not ashamed in Parliament and out of it to make public questions which concern the welfare of millions a mere screen for their own petty private ends, —I say, no fresh scheme of voting will much mend our condition. For take us working men of all sorts. Suppose out of every hundred who had a vote there were thirty who had some soberness, some sense to choose with, some good feeling to make them wish the right thing for all. And suppose there were seventy out of the hundred who were, half of them, not sober, who had no sense to choose one thing in politics more than another, and who had so little good feeling in them that they wasted on their own drinking the money that should have helped to feed and clothe their wives and children; and another half of them who, if they didn't drink, were too ignorant or mean or stupid to see any good for themselves better than pocketing a five shilling piece when it was offered them. Where would be the political power of the thirty sober men? The power would lie with the seventy drunken and stupid votes; and I'll tell you what sort of men would get the power-what sort of men would end by returning whom they pleased to Parliament."

Felix had seen every face around him, and had particularly noticed a recent addition to his audience; but now he looked before him without appearing to fix his glance on any one. In spite of his cooling meditations an hour ago, his pulse was getting quickened by indignation, and the desire to crush what he hated was likely to vent itself in articulation. His tone became more biting.

"They would be men who would undertake to do the business for a candidate, and return him: men who have no real opinions, but who pilfer the words of every opinion, and turn them into a cant which will serve their purpose at the moment; men who look out for dirty work to make their fortunes by, because dirty work wants little talent and no conscience; men who know all the ins and outs of bribery, because there is not a cranny in their own souls where a bribe can't enter. Such men as these will be the masters wherever there's a majority of others who care more for money, more for drink, more for some mean little end which is their own and nobody else's, than for anything that has ever been called Right in the world. For suppose there's a poor voter named Jack, who has seven children, and twelve or fifteen shillings a week wages, perhaps less. Jack can't read—I don't say whose fault that is—he never had the chance to learn; he knows so little that he perhaps thinks God made the poor-laws, and if anybody said the pattern of the workhouse was laid down in the Testament he wouldn't be able to contradict them. What is poor Jack likely to do when he sees a smart stranger coming to him, who happens to be just one of those men that I say will be the masters till public opinion gets too hot for them? He's a middle-sized man, we'll say; stout, with coat upon coat of fine broadcloth, open enough to show a fine gold chain: none of your dark, scowling men, but one with an innocent pink and white skin and very smooth light hair—a most respectable man, who calls himself by a good, sound, well-known English name—as Green, or Baker, or Wilson, or, let us say, Johnson—"

Discussion Questions

1. What criticisms does the first speaker make about the Reform Bill and British politics in general?

2. Why does Felix Holt question the effectiveness of electoral politics and suffrage?

Sources

George Eliot, *Felix Holt*, New York and Chicago: A.L.Burt Company, 1909.

William Baker and Kenneth Womack, eds. *Felix Holt, The Radical*, Peterborough, Ontario: Broadview Press, 2000.

CHAPTER 19

Garibaldi

Memoirs

GARIBALDI, *MEMOIRS*

Garibaldi is still hailed as a hero in both the New and the Old World for his courageous role in nationalist causes on both sides of the Atlantic. Giuseppe Garibaldi was born in Nice in 1807 to a family of sailors and shipowners originally from Genoa. Like his brothers before him, Garibaldi went to sea at a young age, working on ships that plied the French and Italian coastline. He also journeyed to Constantinople and was promoted while still a young man, sometimes captaining ships and other times working as first mate.

Meanwhile, the Italian *Risorgimento* developed into a movement for unification and resistance to first to Napoleonic rule and then later, the conservative rule of the papal states. When Napoleon was defeated, the radical nationalists came to the fore in the struggle for national unification. Garibaldi joined the revolutionary movement and became a disciple of another renowned Italian nationalist, Mazzini. When Garibaldi's revolutionary activities made remaining in Europe dangerous, he sailed for Rio de Janeiro in 1835. While in exile, Garibaldi worked for several South American governments. After a brief stint with the Brazilian government, he served as Commander-in-Chief of the Naval Forces of the Republic of Uruguay from 1842-1848. Upon his return to Europe, Garibaldi led the famous Red Shirts in the conquest of Sicily and then Naples. Garibaldi and his forces pressed toward Rome, but ultimately ceded control over the newly unified territory to the leadership of Victor Emmanuel of Piedmont.

Garibaldi's *Memoirs* were compiled and translated several times. The translation below was taken from the German version published by his mistress, Elpis Melena. Born Marie Espérance von Brandt, eleven years after Garibaldi's birth, in England, Melena spent little time in her birthplace after her childhood. She was forced to marry against her will at the age of 15. Her first husband committed suicide a few years later, freeing the young woman from this unhappy burden. Her second husband shared her passion for travel, but little else. When she opted to become a writer under the pseudonym Elpis Melena, meaning Black Hope, she and her second husband parted ways. Melena took up residence in Rome after 1849, where Garibaldi, the daring Republican freedom fighter, won her heart. Their friendship spanned twenty years, and in that time, Melena aided Garibaldi by acting as his spy, translator, and publicist. In the excerpts that follow, Garibaldi explains how he arrived in the Americas and then relates some of his adventures while in the employ of Brazil and Uruguay.

MEMOIRS

Garibaldi

YOUNG ITALY

From earliest youth I was an enthusiastic admirer of Italy and my most ardent wish was to be initiated into the secrets of her political rebirth, as well as into all books and writings which dealt with Italian freedom, seeking at the same time men who were devoted to serve her. The first one who gave me some information about the course of our patriotic cause was a young Ligurian whom I met on a trip to Taganrog. Truly Columbus himself could not have found greater satisfaction in the discovery of America than I, when it was granted to me to find a man whose mind was turned towards freeing the country, and who assured me that thousands of others were also working on the liberation. From that moment on, my life had a purpose. I became completely absorbed in the national effort, although I felt that it had always been part of me.

On another trip I made aboard the *Clorinde*, I met a number of St. Simonists whom Emile Barrault was taking to Constantinople. I approached the leader, introducing myself as an Italian patriot, and was initiated by him into the ideas of the sect of St. Simonists, who had until then been unknown to me. The conversations with Barrault were not without influence on my ideas, so that the cosmopolitan theories of St. Simonism swept away the one-sided view of my patriotism, and led my gaze from nationality towards humanity.

In 1833 I returned from the Orient to Marseille.

At that time the insurrections of upper and middle Italy had just been betrayed to the governments. Spies had sneaked in among the insurrectionists, and the Piedmont police was working full time. Many people were arrested, while military tribunals condemned 76 conspirators to heavy punishment and 12 death sentences were carried out. But the blood of the martyrs aroused only feelings of revenge, and Mazzini quickly decided to risk a new attempt at insurrection.

The expedition undertaken from Switzerland into Savoy is already known, as well as its failure, thanks to the incompetence, or cowardice, of Ramorino. I had been given a part in the movement which was to follow this expedition. In Marseille I had become friendly with a person named Covi, who introduced me to Mazzini and had announced that I could be relied upon. I joined the Piedmontese Navy as a seaman first class on the frigate *Eurydice*. My task was to proselytize among the crew and if the movement should succeed, I, along with my companions, were to take over the frigate and put it at the disposal of the Republicans.

My propaganda on the *Eurydice* was successful, but despite my burning eagerness, the operations assigned to me did not suffice. In the meantime I found out that in the harbor of Genoa, where we were anchored, an insurrection was about to take place and that the police barracks on Sarzana Square were to be seized. Consequently I left the taking over of the frigate to my companions, put to sea in a boat at the house where the revolt was to start, and landed at the customs. From there I rushed to Sarzana Square.

I waited about an hour, but in vain; there was no gathering of people. Then I heard that the affair had failed, that arrests had been made, and that the Republicans had fled. Thus, since I had joined the Sardinian Navy only in order to further the Republican cause, I thought it useless to return aboard my frigate. Instead I began to ponder my own flight to safety, especially as troops approached and began to encircle the Square. There was no time to lose.

I fled into a fruit shop and confessed my difficult situation to the owner. The excellent woman did not hesitate. She hid me in an installation in the rear, got me some peasant's clothes, and at seven in the evening of February 5, 1834 I left the city of Genoa via the Lanterna Gate disguised as a farmer, proscribed.

Without knowing the way, I turned towards the mountains. Luckily I managed to escape through gardens and over walls, then taking Cassiopea as my guiding star I made my way into the mountains of Sestri. After a march of 10 days, or rather of 10 nights, I reached Nizza. Here I went straight to the house of my aunt and begged her to inform my mother of my arrival, lest she become unduly frightened. I rested a day in Nizza and the following night set off with two friends, Joseph Jauno and Angelo Gustavini. When we came to the Var River we found it swollen by continued rains. My friends remained behind while I swam across to safety.

Now confidently I approached a customs post, told the soldiers my name and why I left Genoa. To my dismay they immediately proclaimed me their prisoner and was placed in custody until further instructions came from Paris. Eventually I was taken to Grasse and from there to Draguignan. In the latter place I escaped from my captors. It happened as I was being led to a room on the first floor where there was a window looking out onto a garden, and as I approached the window and noticed that it was open, I jumped out. The soldiers however, in order to catch me, preferred going down the long way via the staircase. By that time I had reached the street and scurried into the mountains.

I decided to head for Marseille although I had no idea of the route to take. Nevertheless being a sailor, I orientated myself by means of the stars. On the way I came to a village, whose name I no longer recall, and entered an inn and asked for some food. The table was being laid for supper and the young innkeeper and his wife asked me to join them. I readily accepted, found the food and wine good, the fire warm and cozy, my hosts apparently trustful so that I felt safe enough to relate to them my flight and the reasons which motivated it.

To my astonishment the face of the innkeeper darkened as I spoke, so much so, that I enquired about his uneasiness. In brief he explained that he was obliged to arrest me, upon which I laughed, so as to show him that I did not take his threat seriously. Also I was not for a moment afraid, being one against one. "Ah," I finally asked calmly, "you want to arrest me? Very well, I guess after dinner there will be plenty of time for that. Allow me to finish my meal, then I shall pay you double." With that I rattled the coins in my pocket, then continued eating, without appearing worried in the least.

But soon I observed that the innkeeper would have no lack of helpers to secure my arrest. Young people from the village came in, good friends of the innkeeper who came to play cards, drink and sing. The innkeeper now merely kept an eye on me and spoke no more of arrest, obviously relying upon these fellows if necessary, since there must have been at least 10 of them.

A good idea saved me. As one of the drinking fellows finished singing and while the resultant bravos subsided, I quickly raised my glass and exclaimed: "Let me sing also," and I began to sing Beranger's *God of Good People*. I ascribe it not to my passable tenor voice, but to the verses of Beranger, the popularity of the poet, the fraternal spirit of the refrain, and perhaps the pleasant manner in which I sang, that all the audience was carried away. In fact I was obliged to repeat two or three stanzas; then the company finally embraced me and shouted: "Long live Beranger! Long live France! Long live Italy!"

After that there was no more talk of arresting me. My host ignored the matter completely. Instead for the remainder of the entire night we sang, played and drank. At daybreak the whole of that pleasant company offered to accompany me and we parted only after a walk of several hours.

During this journey I also saw for the first time my name in print. It was my death sentence published in the newspaper *Le Peuple souverain* of Marseille.

WANDERINGS

After living a few months in Marseille in idleness under the assumed name of Pane, I was accepted by captain Francesco Gazan and embarked again aboard the ship *Unione* as second in command.

One evening as I had just dressed up to go ashore, I was suddenly aroused by a noise in the water and rushed, followed by the captain, on deck. An unfortunate chap was drowning under the stern of our ship. I jumped into the water, and in sight of a cheering crowd, succeeded in rescuing the young Frenchman from the water and from premature death. The saved one was a fourteen-year-old boy named Joseph Rambaud. His mother was so grateful that her tears wet my cheeks, while the felicitous blessing of the whole family was bestowed upon me. In the port of Smyrna a few years previous I was equally fortunate in saving my friend Claudio Terese.

I pass over the trips which I made aboard the *Unione* to the Black Sea, another later aboard a frigate of war built for the Bey of Tunis from Marseille to Tunis, and finally one aboard a brigantine from Nantes under a Captain Beauregard in a voyage from Marseille to Rio Janeiro. I stopped for the last time in Marseille when I returned from Tunis on a Tunisian brig of war. The city was at that time infested with cholera which brought terrible devastations. Ambulances were set up and many people volunteered their services. I also signed up with one of them, occupying myself for the few days of my stay in Marseille with watching and taking care of cholera patients every night.

On arriving in Rio Janeiro I did not have much time to look for friends. Still without seeking I found one. Rossetti, whom I had never seen before, met me on the *Largo do Passo;* our gaze met, and it seemed as if it were not for the first time. We smiled at each other, and we became brothers, inseparably and for life! I mention elsewhere the warm loving soul of this individual, but I wonder whether I shall die without having been lucky enough to plant a cross in the soil of America where the bones of that noblest and warmest friend of my country lie.

After spending some months in idleness, we decided to begin a trading business. But neither Rossetti nor I seemed born traders. So soon tired of this undertaking, we decided to accept a proposal of Zambeccari, who was secretary to Bento Goncalves, President of the Republic of Rio Grande. The secretary, as well as the President, were Brazilian prisoners of war and imprisoned in Santa Cruz, a fort at the entrance of the harbor of Rio. Zambeccari introduced us to the President, and he gave us letters of marque against Brazil. We outfitted for fighting a small vessel of about 30 tons, the *Mazzini,* with which we had plied our coast-wide trade, and went to sea.

A SOLDIER'S LIFE

In the many storms of my life there has been no lack of fine moments. Such it was as I, at the head of the small group of men who remained after so many battles and who rightfully deserved the name of heroes, rode at the side of my beloved Anita, now the admiration of the whole world. I moved towards a new career which was almost more tempting to me than life at sea.

What did I care that I owned no other clothes than those I had on my back? What did I care that I served a poor republic which could not pay anybody? I had nothing but a sabre and a carbine which I carried over my saddle. My treasure was my Anita, who was aflame no less than I for the holy cause of the people. She had conceived battles as a pleasure and the hardships of the soldier's life as a pastime. Whatever then might come, the future was smiling at us; and the more wild the endless American steppes extended before us, the more pleasant and beautiful they seemed to us. It was a comfort to me to know that in all battles and warlike activities I had done my duty to the best of my ability.

We retreated to Torres on the border of the two provinces and pitched camp. The enemy, content with the taking of the lagoon, did not pursue us. In agreement however with the Division Andrea, the Division Acunha approached via the Serra, having come from the province São Paulo and turned towards Cima de Serra, a mountainous terrain belonging to the province of Rio Grande.

The inhabitants of the Serra, overrun by a superior force, begged General Canabarro for help; he sent out an expedition under the command of Colonel Teixeira to assist them. We also took part in this expedition and, with the people of the Serra assembled under the chief command of Colonel Aranha, we completely defeated the enemy troops near Santa Vittoria. The enemy general lost his life on the River Pelotas, and the greater part of his troops fell into our hands. This victory subdued for the Republican banner the three districts of Lages, Vacaria and Cima de Serra. A few days later we entered Lages triumphantly.

In the meantime in Misiones, as a result of the enemy invasion, the Imperial party had gotten into power again, and Colonel Melo had been able to increase his corps in that province by about 500 cavalry. General Bento Manuel, who was sent against him, could not reach him, since Melo had retreated in the direction of San Paolo, where First Lieutenant Portinhos was also supposed to pursue him. Our position and power would have enabled us not only to resist a thrust of Melo, but also to annihilate completely his whole following. But it was not to be; Colonel Teixeira, not sure whether the enemy would come via Vacaria or via Coritibani, divided his troops into two parts and sent Colonel Aranha with the good cavalry from the Serra to Vacaria, while he himself, with the infantry and a cavalry consisting mainly of prisoners, marched to Coritibani. It was also this direction which the enemy took. But the splintering of our troops was soon fatal to us. Our recently won victory, the impudent character of our commander and our information concerning the state of the enemy, whom we thought to be powerless and demoralized, made us look down upon him with pride and disdain.

After a three-day march we reached Coritibani and took up positions not far from the Pass of Maromba, through which in our opinion the enemy must pass. Along the way, and also on all side roads, sentinels were placed. Towards midnight the sentinel in the pass itself was attacked by the enemy and with such fury that he barely was able to save himself after exchanging a few gun shots. We were ready for the battle. At dawn the enemy approached, crossed the River Maromba and took up his position not far at all from ours.

Realizing the superiority of the enemy, anybody else but Teixeira would have tried at once to bring about a reunion with the column of Aranha while attempting to hold off the enemy at any cost until then; but the hotheaded Republican seemed to fear that the enemy, and with him a fine opportunity to vanquish him, would escape. "To the attack!" he cried, unconcerned about the advantageous position of his opponent. The latter, in using the unevenness of the terrain, had posted himself in battle order on a rather high hill, in front of which a valley opened which was deep and unpassable because of underbrush. On his flanks he posted several cavalry squadrons and in such a way that we could not see them. Teixeira ordered him attacked with an infantry column and believed he could take advantage of the difficult terrain of the valley. The attack took place and the enemy made a semblance of retreat, but while our column, after crossing the valley chased the enemy under violent fire up the hill, it was suddenly attacked on its flank by one of those hidden squadrons, and was obliged to retire in extreme disorder. One of our most able officers paid for this encounter with his life. In spite of this, our column assembled again, and more ready and decided for battle than before, proceeded to the second attack.

This time the enemy really withdrew, leaving one dead behind. There were not many wounded, since altogether only few troops were involved. We pursued the enemy fleeing in wild flight for nine miles with continuous artillery bombardment, for our infantry, even in forced marches, had not been able to continue the pursuit very long.

After reaching the Maromba Pass, we found out from the commander of our advanced guard, Major Giacinto, that the enemy was in the greatest haste to transport his *ganado* and *cavalladas* across the river, in our opinion a sure sign that his flight was meant seriously.

A CATTLE HERDER

So after a *condottiere* I became a cattle herder!

In an estancia named Corral de Pedras I succeeded, with the permission of the Finance Minister, to round up 900 cattle in about twenty days; and if it had been difficult to gather such a number, it was much more difficult to lead the herd to Montevideo.

Innumerable obstacles I had to overcome during my journey; the very worst was the flooded Rio Negro, where I came close to losing my whole capital. Then, in spite of my inexperience and the cheating of my helpers, whom I hired for the transport of the cattle, I saved about 500 head; these however, exhausted by the long trek, the lack of food and the hardships of crossing the river, were deemed incapable of reaching Montevideo. It was therefore decided to slaughter these animals in order, at least, to be able to use their hides, for which the natives have their own word *cuerear*.

After a 50 days' journey, which had become unpleasant to me because of difficulties of all kinds, the cold, hardships and accidents, I finally reached Montevideo with a few hides, the only remnant of my 900 cattle and from which I could clear only a few hundred scudi, just enough to take care of the most necessary needs of my family. In Montevideo I stayed at the home of my friend Napoleone Castellini, who was very kind to me; also at that time I owed much to my other friends there, such as Cuneo, Antonini and Risso. I was in the situation of having to look out for the living costs of three persons, without having the means to do so. The bread of others has always tasted bitter to me, although often in my changing life I have had to take refuge in another's aid and luckily always found friends who offered it to me.

I finally decided on two occupations; they did not bring me much profit, still they assured me a living for some time. I became a broker, and on the side I taught mathematics in the house of Mr. Paolo Semidei; this activity lasted until I joined the Army of the Banda Oriental.

The question of Rio Grande was moving towards a solution, and I could do nothing more for this state, nor could it do any more for me. Soon however I was offered an activity by the Repúdblica Oriental which was more suited to my nature, namely as commander of the war corvette *Constitución*. This brought me into conflict with the Republic of Buenos Aires.

The fleet of the Oriental Republic was commanded by Colonel Coe, the enemy fleet by General Brown, and already some skirmishes, even if indecisive, had taken place. But at the same time a man like Vidal was appointed Minister of the Oriental government, with whom unfortunately only sad memories are connected: in fact, the first thought of this despicable man was to free the Republic of its fleet, declaring it a burden for the state.

This fleet which had cost endless sums and was maintained with all possible care, could have assured at that time an imposing position for that state in the La Plata region; instead, it was ignominiously destroyed by throwing away the wood and remaining materials at unworthy prices.

I was engaged to serve a republic whose lot could only be an unhappy one due to the inexperience and wickedness of the participants.

IN THE SERVICE OF THE REPUBLIC OF URUGUAY

With the *Constitución*, a corvette with 18 cannon, the brigantine *Pereira*, a two-decker also of 18 cannon, and a transport ship, the goelette *Procida*, I was to go to Corrientes, an allied province, to help it in operations of war against Rosas.

Before I continue my narrative however, I think I should first give some explanations about that war and its causes.

The Republic of Uruguay, like almost all South American republics, was torn by inner strife. The cause of it was the jealousy of two generals who vied against each other for the presidency. Fructuoso Rivera, the luckier one, finally succeeded in overthrowing General Manuel Oribe, who had until then held the president's chair. Oribe fled to Buenos Aires where Dictator Rosas received him, as well as other emigrants from Uruguay, and used them against his own enemies at home led by General Lavalle.

In this new situation Rosas saw a desirable opportunity for the realization of his vast plans: namely, to first use Oribe and his followers against Lavalle and thus annihilate the opposing Unitarians at home, who also favored the Rivera regime of the Banda Oriental of Uruguay, then when this was accomplished, to turn the Oribe faction against the Rivera government itself in Montevideo. In this manner Rosas planned to destroy the Uruguayan Republic most surely by injecting it with the germ of a frightful civil war, thus establishing his exclusive supremacy over the entire La Plata region.

At the time I commanded my ship up the La Plata River; the Army of the Republic of Uruguay was San José del Uruguay, while Oribe's army was in Bajada (or Paranti) the capital of the province Entre Rios, and both were preparing for battle. The Army of Corrientes was preparing to unite with that of Uruguay.

I had to ascend the Paraná River as far as Corrientes, a distance of more than 600 miles from Montevideo, along which I could land nowhere except on islands or steppes. The first battle I had to fight since my departure from the capital was against the batteries of Martín García, an island which lies close to the junction of the two large rivers Paraná and Uruguay, and by which one must pass very close, since the surrounding channels are not navigable for large ships. I had some dead and wounded, among others the valiant officer Pocaroba, an Italian, who was decapitated by a cannonball.

Three miles beyond Martín García, the *Constitución* went aground in the sand and unluckily just at the beginning of low tide. It cost us endless trouble to get the ship off again and then to ward off a near annihilation which threatened our small fleet. While we were still occupied in transferring the heavy objects aboard the *Procida*, the enemy fleet appeared on the other side of the island and headed for us under full sails. Never before had I been in so frightful situation: our largest ship aground and lacking its cannon, which now stood on the deck of the *Procida* crammed together in great disorder. Both ships were thus incapacitated for combat and only the *Pereira* remained, whose brave commander with the largest part of his crew had helped us in our labors.

In the meantime the enemy advanced upon us with seven warships, proud and sure of victory amidst the shouts of approval of the island population. My nature does not tend to despair; I have never known this feeling; but that my situation was an embarrassing and painful one everyone can easily judge. It was not only a question of life, for which in that moment I cared little, but also in fighting and dying it was difficult to save our honor, since in our situation it was almost impossible to accept battle. But once again providence held her hand protectively over my fate, and that was enough. The enemy's admiralship also went aground in the sand near the island, and the daring of the enemy was weakened by this. We were saved! The bad luck of our enemy heightened our courage and doubled our strength; within a few hours the *Constitución* was free and could take aboard again her batteries and other material.

"One piece of luck, good or bad, rarely comes alone," so goes the saying. A very dense fog soon enveloped the whole region and did us great service; it hid from the enemy the direction which we took. How much the enemy was mistaken about our route could be seen from the fact that his soldiers pursued us swimming as far as the Uruguay River, into which we had not sailed at all. In this manner the enemy lost many days before he was able to find out exactly the direction we had taken. In the meanwhile I reached the Paraná, protected by the fog and favored by the wind.

I was fully aware of the difficulties of my undertaking while believing that it was the greatest one of my life. But on that day the joy at the surmounted danger and the eagerness for the undertaking itself were no little embittered through the apathy and stubbornness of the pilots. Until that moment they had believed that they were steering towards the Uruguay and pretended not to know the Paraná, hence refused all further responsibility. I really did not care much about their responsibility, what I needed was a pilot, the quicker the better. After a few questions it was learned that some of them actually had knowledge of the river, but were trying to get away from us because they were afraid. However, knowing this was enough; I quickly cleared up all obstacles with my sword. Soon we had a pilot. A favorable wind soon after blew us close to San Nicolás, the first little Argentinian town on the right bank.

There we found several merchant vessels, and since we very urgently needed smaller transport ships and helmsmen, we seized both on a nocturnal expedition. A certain Antonio, an Austrian, who had been trading on the Paraná a long time, fell into our hands as a prisoner and rendered us extraordinary services on our subsequent voyage.

As far as Bajada, where the army of Oribe was, nothing remarkable happened. We landed several times en route to take on fresh provisions which consisted mainly of cattle. This booty was often contested by the inhabitants and by the watchful cavalry, and often some skirmishes occurred which turned out at times good, other times bad. In one of these I lost the excellent officer Vallerga da Loano, a young Italian of extraordinary courage and promising character, who, like so many other sons of Italy, had hoped at some time to shed his blood for the freeing of his unhappy fatherland.

In Bajada, the so-called capital of Entre Rios where the army of Oribe was stationed, we found the most terrible preparations awaiting us, so that before long we were engaged in a battle whose beginning made us fear the worst. However it turned out indecisive, for the favorable wind and our great distance from the enemy batteries made the cannonade, which had already begun, harmless for both parties. In Las Conchas, a few miles above Bajada, we managed a landing which netted us 14 oxen in spite of the most violent resistance of the enemy. Our men fought on this occasion with great bravery, even though the enemy artillery gave us considerable trouble by following us along the shore and using the counterwind, while the narrowness of the river exposed us to their fire for a long time.

In Cerrito, a strong point on the left bank, the enemy had placed a battery of six cannon. The wind was favorable however, but weak, and just at that point blew towards us, because the many windings of the river obliged us often to change direction. We thus had to cover a distance of about two miles under fire from a battery which seemed to hang over our heads.

The battle was brilliant. The largest part of our crew was occupied with the small ships, the others with the cannon; we fought and worked with the utmost cheerfulness, although we had to deal with a proud enemy who had just been victorious and soon after was to defeat the two united armies of Montevideo and Corrientes at the Arroyo Grande. In the meantime we sustained small losses which were easily endured. We had silenced all enemy fire mouths and dislodged several pieces of artillery. Also several merchant ships which had come from Corrientes and Paraguay in order to place themselves under the protection of the enemy battery, fell into our hands.

Discussion Questions

1. What loyalties does Garibaldi express in relating his adventures?
2. How and why did Garibaldi earn the title of hero? What makes him heroic?

Sources

Elpis Melena, *Garibaldi's Memoirs*, Sarasota: International Institute of Garibaldian Studies, 1981.

Jaspar Ridley, *Garibaldi*, New York: The Viking Press, 1976.

CHAPTER 20

Friedrich Nietzsche
Beyond Good and Evil

Cecil Rhodes
"Confession of Faith"

FRIEDRICH NIETZSCHE, *BEYOND GOOD AND EVIL*

Friedrich Nietzsche, one of the towering intellectual figures of the late nineteenth century, was born in a small German town southwest of Leipzig. His father and grandfathers had been Lutheran ministers, and Nietzsche was raised in an atmosphere of piety. The death of his father when Nietzsche was four prompted the family to relocate to Naumburg, where the young boy was raised in a household dominated by women. He attended boarding school in his late teens, and then entered the University of Bonn in 1864, where he studied theology and philology. Groomed to enter the church, Nietzsche shocked his family when he revolted against his spiritual upbringing and instead, embraced a more secular vision of the world. He transferred to the University of Leipzig, where he published his first essays. His rebellions increased as his studies continued. In 1867, Nietzsche began his required military service, but a persistent injury led to his release. Shortly thereafter, the Swiss University of Basel offered Nietzsche a position, despite the fact that he had yet to write a dissertation.

Nietzsche remained at the University of Basel for the next ten years, until his poor health forced him to resign. He cultivated a short-lived friendship with Wagner, who he much admired. He also began to write extensively on German culture. After leaving Basel in 1879, Nietzsche wandered from city to city, returning annually to his mother's house in Naumberg. He wrote prolifically for the next decade, until a mental collapse in 1889 rendered him nearly helpless. His mother and sister cared for him until his death in 1900.

Nietzsche came of age during Bismarck's ascent to power. His life and work embodied the disenchantment of the late nineteenth century. Influenced by the Young Hegelians, Schopenhauer, and Wagner's anti-Semitism, Nietzsche challenged accepted notions of liberalism and rationalism. He also criticized religion, which represented weakness and an obstacle to power and fulfillment in his mind. Nietzsche wrote *Beyond Good and Evil* shortly after publishing his first major attempt to summarize his philosophical outlook, entitled *Thus Spoke Zarathustra*. The first edition of *Beyond Good and Evil* sold more poorly than Nietzsche had anticipated. He did not live to see the text become popular in the early twentieth century. In the passages below, Nietzsche attacks religion and Christianity in particular.

BEYOND GOOD AND EVIL

Nietzsche

45

The human soul and its limits, the range of Inner human experiences reached so far, the heights, depths, and distances of these experiences, the whole history of the soul *so* far and its as yet unexhausted possibilitie—that is the predestined hunting ground for a born psychologist and lover of the "great hunt." But how often he has to say to himself in despair: "One hunter! alas, only a single one! and look at this huge forest, this primeval forest!" And then he wishes he had a few hundred helpers and good, well-trained hounds that he could drive into the history of the human soul to round up *his* game. In vain: It is proved to him again and again, thoroughly and bitterly, how helpers and hounds for all the things that excite his curiosity cannot be found. What is wrong with sending scholars into new and dangerous hunting grounds, where courage, sense, and subtlety in every way are required, is that they cease to be of any use precisely where the *"great hunt,"* but also the great danger, begins: precisely there they lose their keen eye and nose.

To figure out and determine, for example, what kind of a history the problem of *science and conscience* has so far had in the soul of *homines religiosi*, one might perhaps have to be as profound, as wounded, as monstrous as Pascal's intellectual conscience was—and then one would still need that vaulting heaven of bright, malicious spirituality that would be capable of surveying from above, arranging, and forcing into formulas this swarm of danger–ous and painful experiences.

But who would do me this service? But who would have time to wait for such servants? They obviously grow too rarely; they are so improbable in any age. In the end one has to do everything oneself in order to know a few things *oneself:* that is, one has *a lot* to do.

But a curiosity of my type remains after all the most agreeable of all vices—sorry, I meant to say: the love of truth has its reward in heaven and even on earth.—

46

The faith demanded, and not infrequently attained, by original Christianity, in the midst of a skeptical and southern free-spirited world that looked back on, and still contained, a centuries-long fight between philosophical schools, besides the education for tolerance given by the *imperium Romanum*—this faith is *not* that ingenuous and bearlike subalterns' faith with which, say, a Luther or a Cromwell, or some other northern barbarian of the spirit, clung to his god and to Christianity. It is much closer to the faith of Pascal, which resembles in a gruesome manner a continual suicide of reason—a tough, long-lived, wormlike reason that cannot be killed all at once and with a single stroke.

From the start, the Christian faith is a sacrifice: a sacrifice of all freedom, all pride, all self-confidence of the spirit; at the same time, enslavement and self-mockery, self-mutilation. There is cruelty and religious Phoenicianism in this faith which is expected of an over-ripe, multiple, and much-spoiled conscience: it presupposes that the subjection of the spirit *hurts* indescribably; that the whole past and the habits of such a spirit resist the *absurdissimum* which "faith" represents to it.

Modern men, obtuse to all Christian nomenclature, no longer feel the gruesome superlative that struck a classical taste in the paradoxical formula "god on the cross." Never yet and nowhere has there been an equal boldness in inversion, anything as horrible, questioning, and questionable as this formula: it promised a revaluation of all the values of antiquity.

It is the Orient, *deep* Orient, it is the Oriental slave who revenged himself in this way on Rome and its noble and frivolous tolerance, on the Roman "catholicity" of faith. It has always been not faith but the freedom from faith, that half-stoical and smiling unconcern with the seriousness of faith, that enraged slaves in their masters—against their masters. "Enlightenment" enrages: for the slave wants the unconditional; he understands only what is tyrannical, in morals, too; he loves as he hates, without nuance, to the depths, to the point of pain, of sickness—his abundant *concealed* suffering is enraged against the noble taste that seems to *deny* suffering. Nor was skepticism concerning suffering, at bottom merely a pose of aristocratic morality, the least cause of the origin of the last great slave rebellion which began with the French Revolution.

47

Wherever on earth the religious neurosis has appeared we find it tied to three dangerous dietary demands: solitude, fasting, and sexual abstinence. But one cannot decide with certainty what is cause and what effect, and *whether* any relation of cause and effect is involved here. The final doubt seems justified because among its most regular symptoms, among both savage and tame peoples, we also find the most sudden, most extravagant voluptuousness which then, just as suddenly, changes into a penitential spasm and denial of the world and will—both perhaps to be interpreted as masked epilepsy? But nowhere should one resist interpretation more: no other type has yet been surrounded by such a lavish growth of nonsense and superstition, no other type seems to have interested men, even philosophers, more. The time has come for becoming a bit cold right here, to learn caution—better yet: to look away, *to go away*.

Even in the background of the most recent philosophy, that of Schopenhauer, we find, almost as the problem-in-itself, this gruesome question mark of the religious crisis and awakening. How is the denial of the will *possible?* how is the saint possible? This really seems to have been the question over which Schopenhauer became a philosopher and began. And so it was a genuinely Schopenhaucrian conclusion when his most convinced adherent (perhaps also the last one, as far as Germany is concerned), namely, Richard Wagner, finished his life's work at precisely this point and in the end brought this horrible and eternal type on the stage as Kundry, *type vécu*, in the flesh—at the very time when the psychiatrists of almost all the countries of Europe had occasion to study it at close quarters, wherever the religious neurosis—or what I call "*das religiöse Wesen*"—had its latest epidemic outbreak and pageant in the "Salvation Army."

Let us ask what precisely about this whole phenomenon of the saint has seemed so enormously interesting to men of all types and ages, even to philosophers. Beyond any doubt, it was the air of the miraculous that goes with it—namely, the immediate *succession of opposites*, of states of the soul that are judged morally in opposite ways. It seemed palpable that a "bad man" was suddenly transformed into a "saint," a good man. The psychology we have had so far suffered shipwreck at this point: wasn't this chiefly because it had placed itself under the dominion of morals, because it, too, *believed* in opposite moral values and saw, read, *interpreted* these opposites into the text and the facts?

What? The "miracle" merely a mistake of interpretation? A lack of philology?

48

It seems that Catholicism is much more intimately related to the Latin races than all of Christianity in general is to us northerners—and unbelief therefore means something altogether different in Catholic and Protestant countries: among *them,* a kind of rebellion against the spirit of the race, while among us it is rather a return to the spirit (or anti-spirit) of the race. We northerners are undoubtedly descended from barbarian races, which also shows in our talent for religion: we have *little* talent for it. We may except the Celts, who therefore also furnished the best soil for the spread of the Christian infection to the north: in France the Christian ideal came to flourish as much as the pale sun of the north permitted it. How strangely pious for our taste are even the most recent French skeptics insofar as they have any Celtic blood! How Catholic, how un-German Auguste Comte's sociology smells to us with its Roman logic of the instincts! How Jesuitical that gracious and clever cicerone of Port-Royal, Sainte-Beuve, in spite of all his hostility against the Jesuits! And especially Ernest Renan: how inaccessible the language of such a Renan sounds to us northerners: at one instant after another some nothing of religious tension unbalances his soul, which is, in the more refined sense, voluptuous and inclined to stretch out comfortably. Let us speak after him these beautiful sentences—and how much malice and high spirits stir immediately in our probably less beautiful and harder, namely more German, soul as a response!

"So let us make bold to say that religion is a product of the normal man, that man is closest to the truth when he is most religious and most certain of an infinite destiny. . . . It is when he is good that he wants virtue to correspond to an eternal order; it is when he contemplates things in a dis–interested manner that he finds death revolting and absurd. How can we but suppose that it is in moments like this that man sees best?"

These sentences are so utterly *antipodal* to my ears and habits that on finding them my first 'wrath wrote on the margin "*la niaiserie religieuse par excellence!*" But my subsequent wrath actually took a fancy to them—these sentences standing truth on her head! It is so neat, so distinguished to have one's own antipodes!

49

What is amazing about the religiosity of the ancient Greeks is the enormous abundance of gratitude it exudes: it is a very noble type of man that confronts nature and life in *this* way.

Later, when the rabble gained the upper hand in Greece, *fear* became rampant in religion, too—and the ground was prepared for Christianity.—

50

The passion for God: there are peasant types, sincere and obtrusive, like Luther—the whole of Protestantism lacks southern *delicatezza*. There is sometimes an Oriental ecstasy worthy of a slave who, without deserving it, has been pardoned and elevated— for example, in Augustine, who lacks in a truly offensive manner all nobility of gestures and desires. There is a womanly tenderness and lust that presses bashfully and ignorantly toward a *unio mystica et physica*—as in Madame de Guyon. In many cases it appears oddly enough as a disguise for the puberty of a girl or youth, here and there even as the hysteria of an old maid, also as her final ambition—and in several such instances the church has proclaimed the female a saint.

51

So far the most powerful human beings have still bowed worshipfully before the saint as the riddle of self-conquest and deliberate final renunciation. Why did they bow? In him—and as it were behind the question mark of his fragile and miserable appearance—they sensed the superior force that sought to test itself in such a conquest, the strength of the will in which they recognized and honored their own strength and delight in dominion: they honored something in themselves when they honored the saint. Moreover, the sight of the saint awakened a suspicion in them: such an enormity of denial, of anti-nature will not have been desired for nothing, they said to and asked themselves. There may be a reason for it, some very great danger about which the ascetic, thanks to his secret comforters and visitors, might have inside information. In short, the powerful of the world learned a new fear before him; they sensed a new power, a strange, as yet unconquered enemy— it was the "will to power" that made them stop before the saint. They had to ask him—

52

In the Jewish "Old Testament," the book of divine justice, there are human beings, things, and speeches in so grand a style that Greek and Indian literature have nothing to compare with it. With terror and reverence one stands before these tremendous remnants of what man once was, and will have sad thoughts about ancient Asia and its protruding little peninsula Europe, which wants by all means to signify as against Asia the "progress of man." To be sure, whoever is himself merely a meager, tame domestic animal and knows only the needs of domestic animals (like our educated people of today, including the Christians of "educated" Christianity) has no cause for amazement or sorrow among these ruins— the taste for the Old Testament is a touchstone for "great" and "small"—perhaps he will find the *New* Testament, the book of grace, still rather more after his heart (it contains a lot of the real, tender, musty true-believer and small-soul smell). To have glued this New Testament, a kind of rococo of taste in every respect, to the Old Testament to make *one* book, as the "Bible," as "the book par excellence"—that is perhaps the greatest audacity and "sin against the spirit" that literary Europe has on its conscience.

53

Why atheism today?—"The father" in God has been thoroughly refuted; ditto, "the judge," "the rewarder." Also his "free will": he does not hear—and if he heard he still would not know how to help. Worst of all: he seems incapable of clear communication: is he unclear?

This is what I found to be causes for the decline of European theism, on the basis of a great many conversations, asking and listening. It seems to me that the religious instinct is indeed in the process of growing powerfully—but the theistic satisfaction it re- fuses with deep suspicion.

54

What is the whole of modem philosophy doing at bottom? Since Descartes—actually more despite him than because of his precedent—all the philosophers seek to assassinate the old soul concept, under the guise of a critique of the subject-and-predicate concept—which means an attempt on the life of the basic presupposition of the Christian doctrine. Modem philosophy, being an epistemological skepticism, is, covertly or overtly, *anti-Christian*—although, to say this for the benefit of more refined ears, by no means anti-religious.

For, formerly, one believed in "the soul" as one believed In grammar and the grammatical subject: one said, "I" is the condition, "think" Is the predicate and conditioned—thinking is an activity to which thought *must* supply a subject as cause. Then one tried with admirable perseverance and cunning to get out of this net—and asked whether the opposite might not be the case: "think" the condition, "I" the conditioned; "I" in that case only a synthesis which is *made* by thinking. At bottom, *Kant* wanted to prove that, starting from the subject, the subject could not be proved—nor could the object: the possibility of a *merely apparent existence* of the subject, "the sour' in other words, may not always have remained strange to him—that thought which as Vedanta philosophy existed once before on this earth and exercised tremendous power.

Discussion Questions

1. How does Nietzsche characterize Christianity?
2. What, in Nietzsche's opinion, is the alternative to religion?

Sources

Friedrich Nietzsche, *Beyond Good and Evil: Prelude to a Philosophy of the Future*, trans. Walter Kaufmann, New York: Vintage Books, 1989.

Peter Bergmann, *Nietzsche, "the Last Antipolitical German"*,

Bloomington and Indianapolis: Indiana University Press, 1987.

CECIL RHODES
"CONFESSION OF FAITH"

Born in 1853, Cecil Rhodes, the infamous British entrepreneur and colonizer, came from middle class origins. A weak and mediocre child, Rhodes' thirst for money and power brought him successes beyond the scope of his limited natural talents. His father, a reverend, sent the young Rhodes to South Africa in his late teens on the heels of his older brother, who had already received a land grant to cultivate cotton. Rhodes arrived in South Africa in 1870 and soon abandoned cotton farming for the diamond fields, where he took over his brother's claims. His successes were checked by his first heart attack at the age of nineteen, which required eight months away from the fields to recover. Rhodes returned to the diamond mines, however, and began to transform the relations between blacks and whites in the mines. He introduced company mining in the diamond fields, which effectively reduced Africans to laborers, unable to hold their own claims. While dividing his time between Oxford and his interests in South Africa, Rhodes was exposed to the emerging ideology of Social Darwinism, which provided him with justification for his exploitative practices in the mines. He oversaw the founding of the De Beers Mining Company Limited, which would establish a monopoly over the diamond trade. The company implemented repressive labor practices upon its largely black work force, in keeping with Rhodes' increasingly white supremacist politics. Rhodes convinced the crown to grant him a royal charter in 1889, which secured his power over the newly discovered gold fields and greatly expanded British holdings in South Africa. By his mid-thirties, he had become prime minister of Cape Colony, and his personal fortunes continued to grow.

Rhodes' relentless pursuit of racial inequality laid the groundwork for the system of apartheid that crippled South Africa until recent decades. He also bears responsibility for the many lives lost in the Boer War, which he appears to have helped instigate in order to serve his interests in the gold fields of Transvaal. Yet the fame of his fortune inspired countless white settlers to risk their lives in search of similar riches, and his political ascent earned him the reputation of greatness. He virtually controlled British South Africa from 1890 to 1895, and ruled Rhodesia, his namesake, in keeping with his racist outlook. Rhodes revealed those sentiments in his early twenties, when he wrote his "Confession of Faith" at the age of 23 in 1877. In this document, Rhodes professes his beliefs in the superiority of the English and their rights and responsibilities in carving out an empire for Britain.

APPENDIX

Rhodes' "Confession of Faith" of 1877

It often strikes a man to inquire what is the chief good in life; to one the thought comes that it is a happy marriage, to another great wealth, and as each seizes on his idea, for that he more or less works for the rest of his existence. To myself thinking over the same question the wish came to render myself useful to my country. I then asked myself how could I and after reviewing the various methods I have felt that at the present day we are actually limiting our children and perhaps bringing into the world half the human beings we might owing to the lack of country for them to inhabit that if we had retained America there would at this moment be millions more of English living. I contend that we are the finest race in the world and that the more of the world we inhabit the better it is for the human race. Just fancy those parts that are at present inhabited by the most despicable specimens of human beings what an alteration there would be if they were brought under Anglo-Saxon influence, look again at the extra employment a new country added to our dominions gives. I contend that every acre added to our territory means in the future birth to more of the English race who otherwise would not be brought into existence. Added to this the absorption of the greater portion of the world under our rule simply means the end of all wars, at this moment had we not lost America I believe we could have stopped the Russian-Turkish war by merely refusing money and supplies. Having these ideas what scheme could we think of to forward this object. I look into history and I read the story of the Jesuits I see what they were able to do in a bad cause and I might say under bad leaders.

In the present day I become a member in the Masonic order I see the wealth and power they possess the influence they hold and I think over their ceremonies and I wonder that a large body of men can devote themselves to what at times appear the most ridiculous and absurd rites without an object and without an end.

The idea gleaming and dancing before ones eyes like a will-of-the-wisp at last frames itself into a plan. Why should we not form a secret society with but one object the furtherance of the British Empire and the bringing of the whole uncivilised world under British rule for the recovery of the United States for the making the Anglo-Saxon race but one Empire. What a dream, but yet it is probable, it is possible. I once heard it argued by a fellow in my own college, I am sorry to own it by an Englishman, that it was a good thing for us that we have lost the United States. There are some subjects on which there can be no arguments, and to an Englishman this is one of them, but even from an American's point of view just picture what they have lost, look at their government, are not the frauds that yearly come before the public view a disgrace to any country and especially their's which is the finest in the world. Would they have occurred had they remained under English rule great as they have become how infinitely greater they would have been with the softening and elevating influences of English rule, think of those countless ooo's of Englishmen that during the last 100 years would have crossed the Atlantic and settled and populated the United States. Would they have not made without any prejudice a finer country of it than the low class Irish and German emigrants? All this we have lost and that country loses owing to whom? Owing to two or three ignorant pig-headed statesmen of the last century, at their door lies the blame. Do you ever feel mad? do you ever feel murderous. I think I do with those men. I bring facts to prove my assertion. Does an English father when his sons wish to emigrate ever think of suggesting emigration to a country under another flag, never—it would seem a disgrace to suggest such a thing I think that we all think that poverty is better under our own flag than wealth under a foreign one.

Put your mind into another train of thought. Fancy Australia discovered and colonised under the French flag, what would it mean merely several millions of English unborn that at present exist we learn from the past and to form our future. We learn from having lost to cling to what we possess. We know the size of the world we know the total extent. Africa is still lying ready for us it is our duty to take it. It is our duty to seize every opportunity of acquiring more territory and we should keep this one idea steadily before our eyes that more territory simply means more of the Anglo-Saxon race more of the best the most human, most honourable race the world possesses.

To forward such a scheme what a splendid help a secret society would be a society not openly acknowledged but who would work in secret for such an object.

I contend that there are at the present moment numbers of the ablest men in the world who would devote their whole lives to it. I often think what a loss to the English nation in some respects the abolition of the Rotten Borough System has been. What thought strikes a man entering the house of commons, the assembly that rules the whole world? I think it is the mediocrity of the men but what is the cause. It is simply—an assembly of wealth of men whose lives have been spent in the accumulation of money and whose time has been too much engaged to be able to spare any for the study of past history. And yet in the hands of such men rest our destinies. Do men like the great Pitt, and Burke and Sheridan not now exist. I contend they do. There are men now living with I know no other term the mega cscegid of Aristotle but there are not ways for enabling them to serve their Country. They live and die unused unemployed. What has been the main cause of the success of the Romish Church? The fact that every enthusiast, call it if you like every madman finds employment in it. Let us form the same kind of society a Church for the extension of the British Empire. A society which should have its members in every part of the British Empire working with one object and one idea we should have its members placed at our universities and our schools and should watch the English youth passing through their hands just one perhaps in every thousand would have the mind and feelings for such an object, he should be tried in every way, he should be tested whether he is endurant, possessed of eloquence, disregardful of the petty details of life, and if found to be such, then elected and bound by oath to serve for the rest of his life in his Country. He should then be supported if without means by the Society and sent to that part of the Empire where it was felt he was needed.

Take another case, let us fancy a man who finds himself his own master with ample means on attaining his majority whether he puts the question directly to himself or not, still like the old story of virtue and vice in the Memorabilia a fight goes on in him as to what he should do. Take if he plunges into dissipation there is nothing too reckless he does not attempt but after a time his life palls on him, he mentally says this is not good enough, he changes his life, he reforms, he travels, he thinks now I have found the chief good in life, the novelty wears off, and he tires, to change again, he goes into the far interior after the wild game he thinks at last I've found that in life of which I cannot tire, again he is disappointed. He returns he thinks is there nothing I can do in life? Here I am with means, with a good house, with everything that is to be envied and yet I am not happy I am tired of life he possesses within him a portion of the mega cscegid of Aristotle but he knows it not, to such a man the Society should go, should test, and should finally show him the greatness of the scheme and list him as a member.

Take one more case of the younger son with high thoughts, high aspirations, endowed by nature with all the faculties to make a great man, and with the sole wish in life to serve his Country but he lacks two things the means and the opportunity, ever troubled by a sort of inward deity urging him on to high and noble deeds, he is compelled to pass his time in some occupation which furnishes him with mere existence, he lives unhappily and dies miserably. Such men as these the Society should search out and use for the furtherance of their object.

(In every Colonial legislature the Society should attempt to have its members prepared at all times to vote or speak and advocate the closer union of England and the colonies, to crush all disloyalty and every movement for the severance of our Empire. The Society should inspire and even own portions of the press for the press rules the mind of the people. The Society should always be searching for members who might by their position in the world by their energies or character forward the object but the ballot and test for admittance should be severe.)

Once make it common and it fails. Take a man of great wealth who is bereft of his children perhaps having his mind soured by some bitter disappointment who shuts himself up separate from his neighbours and makes up his mind to a miserable existence. To such men as these the society should go gradually disclose the greatness of their scheme and entreat him to throw in his life and property with them for this object. I think that there are thousands now existing who would eagerly grasp at the opportunity. Such are the heads of my scheme.

For fear that death might cut me off before the time for attempting its development I leave all my worldly goods in trust to S. G. Shippard and the Secretary for the Colonies at the time of my death to try to form such a Society with such an object.

Discussion Questions

1. Why, according to Rhodes, are the English superior?
2. How did Rhodes' ideology reflect the realities of imperialism among the European powers in the late nineteenth century?

Sources

John Flint, *Cecil Rhodes*, Boston and Toronto: Little, Brown and Company: 1974.

Antony Thomas, *Rhodes*, New York: St. Martin's Press, 1996.

CHAPTER 21

Charles Darwin
The Origin of Species

Elizabeth Gaskell
Mary Barton

CHARLES DARWIN,
THE ORIGIN OF SPECIES

Charles Darwin hesitated to choose a profession for most of his youth. An average student, he did demonstrate a passion for collecting early in his life, assembling quantities of minerals and insects, but always obeyed his father's directives about choosing a career. His efforts to follow in his father's footsteps and become a doctor failed. By the end of his second year studying in Edinburgh, Darwin realized that his father would leave him a small inheritance, and he began to spend time in the company of a group of young scientists interested in the natural world. His father then sent him to trained as a clergyman at Christ's College, Cambridge. Darwin muddled through his exams, but devoted much of his free time learning about natural science from the small community of professors and students at Cambridge. In 1831, he graduated, and returned home with every intention of finding a position as a country cleric.

When Darwin arrived at his family home, he found two letters, inviting him to join a scientific expedition to explore the coast of Tierra del Fuego, the South Sea Islands, and the Indian Archipelago. Darwin set sail on the *Beagle* in late December 1831. The journey marked a dramatic change in the course of the budding naturalist's life. Geology preoccupied most of his attention during the first leg of the journey, but when the ship arrived in the Galapagos islands in 1835, the creatures that Darwin observed piqued his interest. Further examination of the fossils that he had collected prompted him to ruminate more on the slight differences that he had observed among the same species in the islands. Poor health delayed the writing of *The Origin of Species*, as did his marriage to Emma Wedgwood in 1838. However, marriage also freed him from the responsibility of earning a living, and Darwin turned his attentions to his scientific pursuits. He consulted his colleagues and painstakingly labored over drafts of his theory.

The book's publication in 1859 triggered further debate on the issue of evolution, although Darwin avoided the incendiary topic of human evolution until *The Descent of Man* was published in 1871. Nonetheless, his work provoked an outcry from religious authorities. Others appropriated his theory and used it to justify inequalities among people. Social Darwinism provided the foundations for scientific racism and eugenics in the late nineteenth and early twentieth centuries. In the passage below, taken from *The Origin*, Darwin summarizes his findings in the passage below and refutes the arguments against his theory of natural selection.

THE ORIGIN OF SPECIES

Charles Darwin

CHAPTER XV

As this whole volume is one long argument, it may be convenient to the reader to have the leading facts and inferences briefly recapitulated.

That many and serious objections may be advanced against the theory of descent with modification, through variation and Natural Selection, I do not deny. I have endeavoured to give to them their full force. Nothing at first can appear more difficult to believe than that the more complex organs and instincts have been perfected, not by means superior to, though analogous with, human reason, but by the accumulation of innumerable slight variations, each good for the individual possessor. Nevertheless, this difficulty, though appearing to our imagination insuperably great, cannot be considered real if we admit the following propositions, namely, that all parts of the organization and instincts offer, at least, individual differences—that there is a Struggle for Existence leading to the preservation of profitable deviations of structure or instinct —and, lastly, that gradations in the state of perfection of each organ may have existed, each good of its kind. The truth of these propositions cannot, I think, be disputed.

It is, no doubt, extremely difficult even to conjecture by what gradations many structures have been perfected, more especially among broken and failing groups of organic beings, which have suffered much extinction; but we see so many strange gradations in nature, that we ought to be extremely cautious in saying that any organ or instinct, or any whole structure, could not have arrived at its present state by many graduated steps. There are, it must be admitted, cases of special difficulty opposed to the theory of Natural Selection; and one of the most curious of these / is the existence in the same community of two or three defined castes of workers or sterile female ants; but I have attempted to show how these difficulties can be mastered.

With respect to the almost universal sterility of species when first crossed, which forms so remarkable a contrast with the almost universal fertility of varieties when crossed, I must refer the reader to the recapitulation of the facts given at the end of the ninth chapter, which seem to me conclusively to show that this sterility is no more a special endowment than is the incapacity of two distinct kinds of trees to be grafted together; but that it is incidental on differences confined to the reproductive systems of the intercrossed species. We see the truth of this conclusion in the vast difference in the results of crossing the same two species reciprocally—that is, when one species is first used as the father and then as the mother. Analogy from the consideration of dimorphic and trimorphic plants clearly leads to the same conclusion, for when the forms are illegitimately united, they yield few or no seed, and their offspring are more or less sterile; and these forms belong to the same undoubted species, and differ from each other in no respect except in their reproductive organs and functions.

Although the fertility of varieties when intercrossed and of their mongrel offspring has been asserted by so many authors to be universal, this cannot be considered as quite correct after the facts given on the high authority of Gärtner and Kölreuter. Most of the varieties which have been experimented on have been produced under domestication; and as domestication (I do not mean mere confinement) almost certainly tends to eliminate that sterility which, judging from analogy, would have affected the parent species if intercrossed, we ought not to expect that domestication would likewise induce sterility in their modified descendants when crossed. This elimination of sterility apparently follows from the same cause which allows our domestic animals to breed freely under diversified circumstances; and this again apparently follows from their having been gradually accustomed to frequent changes in their conditions of life.

A double and parallel series of facts seems to throw much light on the sterility of species, when first crossed, and of their hybrid offspring. On the one side, there is good reason to believe that slight changes in the conditions of life give vigour and fertility to all organic beings. We know also that a cross between the distinct individuals of the same variety, and between distinct varieties, increases the number of their offspring, and certainly gives to them / increased size and vigour. This is chiefly owing to the forms which are crossed having been exposed to somewhat different conditions of life; for I have ascertained by a laborious series of experiments that if all the individuals of the same variety be subjected during several generations to the same conditions, the good derived from crossing is often much diminished or wholly disappears. This is one side of the case. On the other side, we know that species which have long been exposed to nearly uniform conditions, when they are subjected under confinement to new and greatly changed conditions, either perish, or if they survive, are rendered sterile, though retaining perfect health. This does not occur, or only in a very slight degree, with our domesticated productions, which have long been exposed to fluctuating conditions. Hence, when we find that hybrids produced by a cross between two distinct species are few in number, owing to their perishing soon after conception or at a very early age, or if surviving that they are rendered more or less sterile, it seems highly probable that this result is due to their having been in fact subjected to a great change in their conditions of life, from being compounded of two distinct organizations. He who will explain in a definite manner why, for instance, an elephant or a fox will not breed under confinement in its native country, whilst the domestic pig or dog will breed freely under the most diversified conditions, will at the same time be able to give a definite answer to the question why two distinct species, when crossed, as well as their hybrid offspring, are generally rendered more or less sterile, whilst two domesticated varieties when crossed and their mongrel offspring are perfectly fertile.

Turning to geographical distribution, the difficulties encountered on the theory of descent with modification are serious enough. All the individuals of the same species, and all the species of the same genus, or even higher group, are descended from common parents; and therefore, in however distant and isolated parts of the world they may now be found, they must in the course of successive generations have travelled from some one point to all the others. We are often wholly unable even to conjecture how this could have been effected. Yet, as we have reason to believe that some species have retained the same specific form for very long periods of time, immensely long as measured by years, too much stress ought not to be laid on the occasional wide diffusion of the same species; for during very long periods there will always have been a good chance for wide migration by many means. A broken or interrupted range may often be accounted for by the extinction of the species in the intermediate regions. It cannot be denied / that we are as yet very ignorant as to the full extent of the various climatal and geographical changes which have affected the earth during modern periods; and such changes will often have facilitated migration. As an example, I have attempted to show how potent has been the influence of the Glacial period on the distribution of the same and of allied species throughout the world. We are as yet profoundly ignorant of the many occasional means of transport. With respect to distinct species of the same genus inhabiting distant and isolated regions, as the process of modification has necessarily been slow, all the means of migration will have been possible during a very long period; and consequently the difficulty of the wide diffusion of the species of the same genus is in some degree lessened.

As according to the theory of Natural Selection an interminable number of intermediate forms must have existed, linking together all the species in each group by gradations as fine as are our existing varieties, it may be asked, Why do we not see these linking forms all around us? Why are not all organic beings blended together in an inextricable chaos? With respect to existing forms, we should remember that we have no right to expect (excepting in rare cases) to discover *directly* connecting links between them, but only between each and some extinct and supplanted form. Even on a wide area, which has during a long period remained continuous, and of which the climatic and other conditions of life change insensibly in proceeding from a district occupied by one species into another district occupied by a closely allied species, we have no just right to expect often to find intermediate varieties in the intermediate zones. For we have reason to believe that only a few species of a genus ever undergo change; the other species becoming utterly extinct and leaving no modified progeny. Of the species which do change, only a few within the same country change at the same time; and all modifications are slowly effected. I have also shown that the intermediate varieties which probably at first existed in the intermediate zones, would be liable to be supplanted by the allied forms on either hand; for the latter, from existing in greater numbers, would generally be modified and improved at a quicker rate than the intermediate varieties, which existed in lesser numbers; so that the intermediate varieties would, in the long run, be supplanted and exterminated.

On this doctrine of the extermination of an infinitude of connecting links, between the living and extinct inhabitants of the world, and at each successive period between the extinct and still / older species, why is not every geological formation charged with such links? Why does not every collection of fossil remains afford plain evidence of the gradation and mutation of the forms of life? Although geological research has undoubtedly revealed the formner existence of many links, bringing numerous forms of life much closer together, it does not yield the infinitely many fine gradations between past and present species required on the theory; and this is the most obvious of the many objections which may be urged against it. Why, again, do whole groups of allied species appear, though this appearance is often false, to have come in suddenly on the successive geological stages? Although we now know that organic beings appeared on this globe, at a period incalculably remote, long before the lowest bed of the Cambrian system was deposited, why do we not find beneath this system great piles of strata stored with the remains the progenitors of the Cambrian fossils? For on the theory, such strata must somewhere have been deposited at these ancient and utterly unknown epochs of the world's history.

I can answer these questions and objections only on the supposition that the geological record is far more imperfect than most geologists believe. The number of specimens in all our museums is absolutely as nothing compared with the countless generations of countless species which have certainly existed. The parent form of any two or more species would not be in all its characters directly intermediate between its modified offspring, any more than tile rock-pigeon is directly intermediate in crop and tail between its descendants, the pouter and fantail pigeons. We should not be able to recognize a species as the parent of another and modified species, if we were to examine the two ever so closely, unless we possessed most of the intermediate links; and owing to the imperfection of the geological record, we have no just right to expect to find so many links. If two or three, or even more linking forms were discovered, they would simply be ranked by many naturalists as so many new species, more especially if found in different geological sub-stages, let their differences be ever so slight. Numerous existing doubtful forms could be named which are probably varieties; but who will pretend that in future ages so many fossil links will be discovered, that naturalists will be able to decide whether or not these doubtful forms ought to be called varieties? Only a small portion of the world has been geologically explored. Only organic beings of certain classes can be preserved in a fossil condition, at least in any great number. Many species when once formed never undergo any further change but become extinct / without leaving modified descendants; and the periods, during which species have undergone modification, though long as measured by years, have probably been short in comparison with the periods during which they retained the same form. It is the dominant and widely ranging species which vary most frequently and vary most, and varieties are often at first local—both causes rendering the discovery of intermediate links in any one formation less likely. Local varieties will not spread into other and distant regions until they are considerably modified and improved; and when they have spread, and are discovered in a geological formation, they appear as if suddenly created there, and will be simply classed as new species. Most formations have been intermittent in their accumulation; and their duration has probably been shorter than the average duration of specific forms. Successive formations are in most cases separated from each other by blank intervals of time of great length; for fossiliferous formations thick enough to resist future degradation can as a general rule be accumulated only where much sediment is deposited on the subsiding bed of the sea. During the alternate periods of elevation and of stationary level the record will generally be blank. During these latter periods there will probably be more variability in the forms of life; during periods of subsidence, more extinction.

With respect to the absence of strata rich in fossils beneath the Cambrian formation, I can recur only to the hypothesis given in the tenth chapter; namely, that though our continents and oceans have endured for an enormous period in nearly their present relative positions, we have no reason to assume that this has always been the case; consequently formations much older than any now known may lie buried beneath the great oceans. With respect to the lapse of time not having been sufficient since our planet was consolidated for the assumed amount of organic change, and this objection, as urged by Sir William Thompson, is probably one of the gravest as yet advanced, I can only say, firstly, that we do not know at what rate species change as measured by years. and secondly, that many philosophers are not as yet willing to admit that we know enough of the constitution of the universe and of the interior of our globe to speculate with safety on its past duration.

That the geological record is imperfect all will admit; but that it is imperfect to the degree required by our theory, few will he inclined to admit. If we look to long enough intervals of time, geology plainly declares that species have all changed; and they have changed in the manner required by the theory, for they have / changed slowly and in a graduated manner. We clearly see this in the fossil remains from consecutive formations invariably being much more closely related to each other, than are the fossils from widely separated formations.

Such is the sum of the several chief objections and difficulties which may be justly urged against the theory; and I have now briefly recapitulated the answers and explanations which, as far as I can see may be given. I have felt these difficulties far too heavily during many years to doubt their weight. But it deserves especial notice that the more important objections relate to questions on which we are confessedly ignorant; nor do we know how ignorant we are. We do not know all the possible transitional gradations between the simplest and the most perfect organs; it cannot be pretended that we know all the varied means of distribution during the long lapse of years, or that we know how imperfect is the geological record. Serious as these several objections are, in my judgement they are by no means sufficient to overthrow the theory of descent with subsequent modification.

Discussion Questions

1. How does natural selection take place?

2. What kinds of challenges did critics raise regarding Darwin's theory? How successfully did he rebut those objections?

Sources

Paul H. Barrett and R.B. Freeman, eds., *The Works of Charles Darwin*, Vol. 16, New York: New York University Press, 1988.

Gertrude Himmelfarb, *Darwin and the Darwinian Revolution*, Chicago: Ivan R. Dee, Inc., 1996.

ELIZABETH GASKELL, *MARY BARTON*

Born Elizabeth Cleghorn Stevenson in Chelsea, London in 1810, Gaskell was raised by her aunt when her mother died a year after her birth. Hanna Lumb, her aunt, resided in Knutsford, Chesire, just outside of Manchester. As a girl, Gaskell developed an appreciation for natural beauty that she never lost, especially when she came to reside in a thriving yet polluted industrial center. The family agreed to send Gaskell to boarding school at the age of twelve, although she was transferred to a more liberal institution after a year. In 1832, she married a minister and moved to Manchester. When the loss of an infant son resulted in depression in 1845, Gaskell's husband encouraged her to find solace in writing. She first published stories anonymously in several journals, then ventured to write her first novel, *Mary Barton*, also published anonymously. The book went to press in 1848, and several other editions were printed in subsequent years. After the success of the novel, Gaskell wrote another book for which she also earned acclaim, *The Life of Charlotte Brontë*. Despite her own work as a biographer, Gaskell resisted the efforts of her admirers to chronicle her own life.

Gaskell had lived and worked by the side of her husband at the Cross Street Chapel for over a decade and a half when she wrote *Mary Barton*. The novel illustrates the social crisis that characterized the life of working people in the rapidly expanding industrial center in the mid-eighteenth century. Gaskell had come to know Manchester's middle class through her work at the church, but the novel's heroes are ordinary working class people who strive to maintain their dignity under the most crushing circumstances. In the novel, Gaskell traces the downfall of her main character, John Barton. Although Gaskell disapprovingly recounts her character's opium use and trade union activism, she also portrays his plight compassionately. In the following selection, Gaskell explores John

Barton's perspective on the relationship between workers and masters. Although she struggles to portray working class radicalism and the trade union movement in a positive light, Gaskell manages to maintain her empathy for Barton.

MARY BARTON

Elizabeth Gaskell

CHAPTER 15

We must return to John Barton. Poor John! He never got over his disappointing journey to London. The deep mortification he then experienced (with, perhaps, as little selfishness for its cause as mortification ever had) was of no temporary nature; indeed, few of his feelings were.

Then came a long period of bodily privation; of daily hunger after food; and though he tried to persuade himself he could bear want himself with stoical indifference, and did care about it as little as most men, yet the body took its revenge for its uneasy feelings. The mind became soured and morose, and lost much of its equipoise. It was no longer elastic, as in the days of youth, or in times of comparative happiness; it ceased to hope. And it is hard to live on when one can no longer hope.

The same state of feeling which John Barton entertained, if belonging to one who had had leisure to think of such things, and physicians to give names to them, would have been called monomania; so haunting, so incessant, were the thoughts that pressed upon him. I have somewhere read a forcibly described punishment among the Italians, worthy of a Borgia. The supposed or real criminal was shut up in a room, supplied with every convenience and luxury; and at first mourned little over his imprisonment. But day by day he became aware that the space between the walls of his apartment was narrowing, and then he understood the end. Those painted walls would come into hideous nearness, and at last crush the life out of him.

And so day by day, nearer and nearer, came the diseased thoughts of John Barton. They excluded the light of heaven, the cheering sounds of earth. They were preparing his death.

It is true much of their morbid power might be ascribed to the use of opium. But before you blame too harshly this use, or rather abuse, try a hopeless life, with daily cravings of the body for food. Try, not alone being without hope yourself, but seeing all around you reduced to the same despair, arising from the same circumstances; all around you telling (though they use no words or language), by their looks and feeble actions, that they are suffering and sinking under the pressure of want. Would you not be glad to forget life, and its burdens? And opium gives forgetfulness for a time.

It is true they who thus purchase it pay dearly for their oblivion; but can you expect the uneducated to count the cost of their whistle? Poor wretches! They pay a heavy price. Days of oppressive weariness and languor, whose realities have the feeble sickliness of dreams; nights, whose dreams are fierce realities of agony; sinking health, tottering frames, incipient madness, and worse, the *consciousness* of incipient madness; this is the price of their whistle. But have you taught them the science of consequences?

John Barton's overpowering thought, which was to work out his fate on earth, was rich and poor; why are they so separate, so distinct, when God has made them all? It is not His will that their interests are so far apart. Whose doing is it?

And so on into the problems and mysteries of life, until, bewildered and lost, unhappy and suffering, the only feeling that remained clear and undisturbed in the tumult of his heart, was hatred to the one class, and keen sympathy with the other.

But what availed his sympathy? No education had given him wisdom; and without wisdom, even love, with all its effects, too often works but harm. He acted to the best of his judgment, but it was a widely-erring judgment.

The actions of the uneducated seem to me typified in those of Frankenstein, that monster of many human qualities, ungifted with a soul, a knowledge of the difference between good and evil.

The people rise up to life; they irritate us, they terrify us, and we become their enemies. Then, in the sorrowful moment of our triumphant power, their eyes gaze on us with mute reproach. Why have we made them what they are; a powerful monster, yet without the inner means for peace and happiness?

John Barton became a Chartist, a Communist all that is commonly called wild and visionary. Ay! but being visionary is something. It shows a soul, a being, not altogether sensual; a creature who looks forward for others, if not for himself.

And with all his weakness he had a sort of practical power, which made him useful to the bodies of men to whom he belonged. He had a ready kind of rough Lancashire eloquence, arising out of the fulness of his heart, which was very stirring to men similarly circumstanced, who liked to hear their feelings put into words. He had a pretty clear head at times, for method and arrangement; a necessary talent to large combinations of men. And what perhaps more than all made him relied upon and valued, was the consciousness which every one who came in contact with him felt, that he was actuated by no selfish motives; that his class, his order, was what he stood by, not the rights of his own paltry self. For even in great and noble men, as soon as self comes into prominent existence, it becomes a mean and paltry thing.

A little time before this, there had come one of those occasions for deliberation among the employed, which deeply interested John Barton, and the discussions concerning which had caused his frequent absence from home of late.

I am not sure if I can express myself in the technical terms of either masters or workmen, but I will try simply to state the case on which the latter deliberated.

An order for coarse goods came in from a new foreign market. It was a large order, giving employment to all the mills engaged in that species of manufacture; but it was necessary to execute it speedily, and at as low prices as possible, as the masters had reason to believe that a duplicate order had been sent to one of the continental manufacturing towns, where there were no restrictions on food, no taxes on building or machinery, and where consequently they dreaded that the goods could be made at a much lower price than they could afford them for; and that, by so acting and charging, the rival manufactures would obtain undivided possession of the market. It was clearly their interest to buy cotton as cheaply, and to beat down wages as low as possible. And in the long run the interests of the workmen would have been thereby benefited. Distrust each other as they may, the employers and the employed must rise or fall together. There may be some difference as to chronology, none as to fact.

But the masters did not choose to make all these circumstances known. They stood upon being the masters, and that they had a right to order work at their own prices, and they believed that in the present depression of trade, and unemployment of hands, there would be no great difficulty in getting it done.

Now let us turn to the workmen's view of the question. The masters (of the tottering foundation of whose prosperity they were ignorant) seemed doing well, and, like gentlemen, 'lived at home in ease,' while they were starving, gasping on from day to day; and there was a foreign order to be executed, the extent of which, large as it was, was greatly exaggerated; and it was to be done speedily. Why were the masters offering such low wages under these circumstances? Shame upon them! It was taking advantage of their workpeople being almost starved; but they would starve entirely rather than come into such terms. It was bad enough to be poor, while by the labour of their thin hands, the sweat of their brows, the masters were made rich; but they would not be utterly ground down to dust. No! they would fold their hands and sit idle, and smile at the masters, whom even in death they could baffle. With Spartan endurance they determined to let the employers know their power, by refusing to work.

So class distrusted class, and their want of mutual confidence wrought sorrow to both. The masters would not be bullied, and compelled to reveal why they felt it wisest and best to offer only such low wages; they would not be made to tell that they were even sacrificing capital to obtain a decisive victory over the continental manufacturers. And the workmen sat silent and stern with folded hands refusing to work for such pay. There was a strike in Manchester.

Of course it was succeeded by the usual consequences. Many other Trades' Unions, connected with different branches of business, supported with money, countenance, and encouragement of every kind, the stand which the Manchester power-loom weavers were making against their masters. Delegates from Glasgow, from Nottingham, and other towns, were sent to Manchester, to keep up the spirit of resistance; a committee was formed, and all the requisite officers elected; chairman, treasurer, honorary secretary:—among them was John Barton.

The masters, meanwhile, took their measures. They placarded the walls with advertisements for power-loom weavers. The workmen replied by a placard in still larger letters, stating their grievances. The masters met daily in town, to mourn over the time (so fast slipping away) for the fulfilment of the foreign orders; and to strengthen each other in their resolution not to yield. If they gave up now, they might give up always. It would never do. And amongst the most energetic of the masters, the Carsons, father and son, took their places. It is well known, that there is no religionist so zealous as a convert; no masters so stern, and regardless of the interests of their workpeople, as those who have risen from such a station themselves. This would account for the elder Mr Carson's determination not to be bullied into yielding; not even to be bullied into giving reasons for acting as the masters did. It was the employers' will, and that should be enough for the employed. Harry Carson did not trouble himself much about the grounds for his conduct. He liked the excitement of the affair. He liked the attitude of resistance. He was brave, and he liked the idea of personal danger, with which some of the more cautious tried to intimidate the violent among the masters.

Meanwhile, the power-loom weavers living in the more remote parts of Lancashire, and the neighbouring counties, heard of the masters' advertisements for workmen; and in their solitary dwellings grew weary of starvation, and resolved to come to Manchester. Foot-sore, way-worn, half-starved looking men they were, as they tried to steal into town in the early dawn, before people were astir, or in the dusk of the evening. And now began the real wrong-doing of the Trades' Unions. As to their decision to work, or not, at such a particular rate of wages, that was either wise or unwise; all error of judgment at the worst. But they had no right to tyrannise over others, and tie them down to their own Procrustean bed. Abhorring what they considered oppression in the masters, why did they oppress others? Because, when men get excited, they know not what they do. Judge, then, with something of the mercy of the Holy One, whom we all love.

In spite of policemen, set to watch over the safety of the poor country weavers—in spite of magistrates, and prisons, and severe punishments—the poor depressed men tramping in from Burnley, Padiham, and other places, to work at the condemned 'Starvation Prices,' were waylaid, and beaten, and left by the road-side almost for dead. The police broke up every lounging knot of men:—they separated quietly, to reunite half-a-mile out of town.

Of course the feeling between the masters and workmen did not improve under these circumstances.

Combination is an awful power. It is like the equally mighty agency of steam; capable of almost unlimited good or evil. But to obtain a blessing on its labours, it must work under the direction of a high and intelligent will; incapable of being misled by passion or excitement. The will of the operatives had not been guided to the calmness of wisdom.

The day arrived on which the masters were to have an interview with a deputation of the workpeople. The meeting was to take place in a public room, at an hotel; and there, about eleven o'clock, the mill-owners, who had received the foreign orders, began to collect.

Of course, the first subject, however full their minds might be of another, was the weather. Having done their duty by all the showers and sunshine which had occurred during the past week, they fell to talking about the business which brought them together. There might be about twenty gentlemen in the room, including some by courtesy, who were not immediately concerned in the settlement of the present question; but who, nevertheless, were sufficiently interested to attend. These were divided into little groups, who did not seem by any means unanimous. Some were for a slight concession, just a sugar-plum to quieten the naughty child, a sacrifice to peace and quietness. Some were steadily and vehemently opposed to the dangerous precedent of yielding one jot or one tittle to the outward force of a turn-out. It was teaching the workpeople how to become masters, said they. Did they want the wildest thing hereafter, they should know that the way to obtain their wishes would be to strike work. Besides, one or two of those present had only just returned from the New Bailey, where one of the turn-outs had been tried for a cruel assault on a poor north-country weaver, who had attempted to work at the low price. They were indignant, and justly so, at the merciless manner in which the poor fellow had been treated; and their indignation at wrong, took (as it often does) the extreme form of revenge. They felt as if, rather than yield to the body of men who were resorting to such cruel measures towards their fellow-workmen, they, the masters, would sooner relinquish all the benefits to be derived from the fulfilment of the commission, in order that the workmen might suffer keenly. They forgot that the strike was in this instance the consequence of want and need, suffered unjustly as the endurers believed; for, however insane, and without ground of reason, such was their belief, and such was the cause of their violence. It is a great truth that you cannot extinguish violence by violence. You may put it down for a time; but while you are crowing over your imaginary success, see if it does not return with seven devils worse than its former self!

No one thought of treating the workmen as brethren and friends, and openly, clearly, as appealing to reasonable men, stating exactly and fully the circumstances which led the masters to think it was the wise policy of the time to make sacrifices themselves, and to hope for them from the operatives.

In going from group to group in the room, you caught such a medley of sentences as the following:

'Poor devils! they're near enough to starving, I'm afraid. Mrs Aldred makes two cows' heads into soup every week, and people come many miles to fetch it; and if these times last, we must try and do more. But we must not be bullied into any thing!'

'A rise of a shilling or so won't make much difference, and they will go away thinking they've gained their point.'

'That's the very thing I object to. They'll think so, and whenever they've a point to gain, no matter how unreasonable, they'll strike work.'

'It really injures them more than us.'

'I don't see how our interests can be separated.'

'The d—d brute had thrown vitriol on the poor fellow's ankles, and you know what a bad part that is to heal. He had to stand still with the pain, and that left him at the mercy of the cruel wretch, who beat him about the head till you'd hardly have known he was a man. They doubt if he'll live.'

'If it were only for that, I'll stand out against them, even if it is the cause of my ruin.

'Ay, I for one won't yield one farthing to the cruel brutes; they're more like wild beasts than human beings.'

(Well, who might have made them different?)

'I say, Carson, just go and tell Duncombe of this fresh instance of their abominable conduct. He's wavering, but I think this will decide him.

The door was now opened, and the waiter announced that the men were below, and asked if it were the pleasure of the gentlemen that they should be shown up.

They assented, and rapidly took their places round the official table; looking, as like as they could, to the Roman senators who awaited the irruption of Brennus and his Gauls.

Tramp, tramp, came the heavy clogged feet up the stairs; and in a minute five wild, earnest-looking men, stood in the room. John Barton, from some mistake as to time, was not among them. Had they been larger boned men, you would have called them gaunt; as it was, they were little of stature, and their fustian clothes hung loosely upon their shrunk limbs. In choosing their delegates, too, the operatives had had more regard to their brains, and power of speech, than to their wardrobes; they might have read the opinions of that worthy Professor Teufelsdreck, in Sartor Resartus, to judge from the dilapidated coats and trousers, which yet clothed men of parts and of power. It was long since many of them had known the luxury of a new article of dress; and air-gaps were to be seen in their garments. Some of the masters were rather affronted at such a ragged detachment coming between the wind and their nobility; but what cared they?

At the request of a gentleman hastily chosen to officiate as chairman, the leader of the delegates read, in a high-pitched, psalm-singing voice, a paper, containing the operatives' statement of the case at issue, their complaints, and their demands, which last were not remarkable for moderation.

He was then desired to withdraw for a few minutes, with his fellow-delegates, to another room, while the masters considered what should be their definitive answer.

When the men had left the room, a whispered earnest consultation took place, every one re-urging his former arguments. The conceders carried the day, but only by a majority of one. The minority haughtily and audibly expressed their dissent from the measures to be adopted, even after the delegates reentered the room; their words and looks did not pass unheeded by the quick-eyed operatives; their names were registered in bitter hearts.

The masters could not consent to the advance demanded by the workmen. They would agree to give one shilling per week more than they had previously offered. Were the delegates empowered to accept such offer?

They were empowered to accept or decline any offer made that day by the masters.

Then it might be as well for them to consult among themselves as to what should be their decision. They again withdrew.

It was not for long. They came back, and positively declined any compromise of their demands.

Then up sprang Mr Henry Carson, the head and voice of the violent party among the masters, and addressing the chairman, even before the scowling operatives, he proposed some resolutions, which he, and those who agreed with him, had been concocting during this last absence of the deputation.

They were, firstly, withdrawing the proposal just made, and declaring all communication between the masters and that particular Trades' Union at an end; secondly, declaring that no master would employ any workman in future, unless he signed a declaration that he did not belong to any Trades' Union, and pledged himself not to assist or subscribe to any society, having for its object interference with the masters' powers; and, thirdly, that the masters should pledge themselves to protect and encourage all workmen willing to accept employment on those conditions, and at the rate of wages first offered. Considering that the men who now stood listening with lowering brows of defiance were all of them leading members of the Union, such resolutions were in themselves sufficiently provocative of animosity: but not content with simply stating them, Harry Carson went on to characterise the conduct of the workmen in no measured terms; every word he spoke rendering their looks more livid, their glaring eyes more fierce. One among them would have spoken, but checked himself in obedience to the stern glance and pressure on his arm, received from the leader. Mr Carson sat down, and a friend instantly got up to second the motion. It was carried, but far from unanimously. The chairman announced it to the delegates (who had been once more turned out of the room for a division). They received it with deep brooding silence, but spake never a word, and left the room without even a bow.

Discussion Questions

1. What kinds of anxieties do you detect in Gaskell's representation of the trade union movement and the agitation of the working classes in eighteenth century Britain?

2. What kinds of social, economic, and political transformations do Gaskell's descriptions of life in Manchester reflect?

Sources

Elizabeth Gaskell, *Mary Barton*, London: J.M. Dent, 1996.

Winifred Gérin, *Elizabeth Gaskell: A Biography*, Oxford: Clarendon Press, 1976.

CHAPTER 22

John Reed
Ten Days that Shook the World

Erich Maria Remarque
All Quiet on the Western Front

JOHN REED, *TEN DAYS THAT SHOOK THE WORLD*

The American journalist and writer John Reed was born in Portland, Oregon in 1887. The grandson of a pioneer capitalist and the son of a businessman from the east coast, Reed enjoyed a privileged childhood in the family mansion until his parents encountered financial difficulties caused by the ups and downs of the economy in the last decade of the nineteenth century. As a child, Reed sought refuge from the frailty caused by a recurring kidney ailment in books, mostly fiction. After attending an exclusive institution in Portland and a prep school back east, Reed entered Harvard. Reed threw himself into writing, penning verses for a humorous magazine at first, then publishing stories in the more prestigious *Harvard Monthly*. He graduated in 1910, and traveled to Europe. Reed booked passage on a British freighter and worked as nightwatchman, enjoying the boisterous company of the sailors. After a year abroad, Reed returned to New York, where he struggled to make ends meet as a writer. His efforts paid off when he landed an editorship at the *American*. After the death of his father, he immersed himself in the radical vibrancy of New York's Greenwich Village and accepted a position at *The Masses*, a left-leaning publication. His sympathies for the IWW landed him in jail, an experience that stiffened his increasingly partisan views.

In 1913, as revolution erupted in Mexico, Reed jumped at the opportunity to cover the conflict. His interview with Pancho Villa completed his conversion to revolutionary politics. Reed chronicled the upheaval of revolution in *Insurgent Mexico*. The book earned him instant credibility in revolutionary circles. Reed's next major assignment gave him little joy. Covering the destruction of World War I violated his sense of hope. A tour of eastern Europe after the war left him even more disheartened. The Russian revolution launched in the spring of 1917 reinvigorated his enthusiasm. Writing for an audience hostile to the communist outlook of the Bolsheviks, Reed portrayed the revolution as the unavoidable culmination of historical processes. He passionately endorsed the events occurring in 1917, with little concern for the consequences for himself or the possibility that the dream of a more egalitarian society might remain unfulfilled. The persecution of leftists in the U.S. made it nearly impossible for Reed to publish his pieces after his reporting on the Russian revolution. He retreated into the world of writing, pounding out *Ten Days that Shook the World* in two months. In the dramatic passage below, Reed describes the role of the Bolsheviks in launching the revolution and the forces of opposition that stood in their way.

TEN DAYS THAT SHOOK THE WORLD

John Reed

Since March, 1917, when the roaring torrents of workmen and soldiers beating upon the Tauride Palace compelled the reluctant Imperial Duma to assume the supreme power in Russia, it was the masses of the people, workers, soldiers and peasants, which forced every change in the course of the Revolution. They hurled the Miliukov Ministry down; it was their Soviet which proclaimed to the world the Russian peace terms—"No annexations, no indemnities, and the right of self-determination of peoples"; and again, in July, it was the spontaneous rising of the unorganised proletariat which once more stormed the Tauride Palace, to demand that the Soviets take over the Government of Russia.

The Bolsheviki, then a small political sect, put themselves at the head of the movement. As a result of the disastrous failure of the rising, public opinion turned against them, and their leaderless hordes slunk back into the Viborg Quarter, which is Petrograd's *St. Antoine.* Then followed a savage hunt of the Bolsheviki; hundreds were imprisoned, among them Trotzky, Madame Kollontai and Kameniev; Lenin and Zinoviev went into hiding, fugitives from justice; the Bolshevik papers were suppressed. Provocators and reactionaries raised the cry that the Bolsheviki were German agents, until people all over the world believed it.

But the Provisional Government found itself unable to substantiate its accusations; the documents proving pro-German conspiracy were discovered to be forgeries ;* and one by one the Bolsheviki were released from prison without trial, on nominal or no bail—until only six remained. The impotence, and indecision of the ever-changing Provisional Government was an argument nobody could refute. The Bolsheviki raised again the slogan so dear to the masses, "All Power to the Soviets !"—and they were not merely self-seeking, for at that time the majority of the Soviets was "moderate" Socialist, their bitter enemy.

* Part of the famous "Sisson Documents."

But more potent still, they took the crude, simple desires of the workers, soldiers and peasants, and from them built their immediate programme. And so, while the *oborontsi* Mensheviki and Socialist Revolutionaries involved themselves in compromise with the bourgeoisie, the Bolsheviki rapidly captured the Russian masses. In July they were hunted and despised; by September the metropolitan workmen, the sailors of the Baltic Fleet, and the soldiers, had been won almost entirely to their cause. The September municipal elections in the large cities were significant; only 18 per cent of the returns were Menshevik and Socialist Revolutionary, against more than 70 per cent in June. . . .

There remains a phenomenon which puzzled foreign observers: the fact that the Central Executive Committees of the Soviets, the Central Army and Fleet Committees,* and the Central Committees of some of the Unions—notably, the Post and Telegraph Workers and the Railway Workers—opposed the Bolsheviki with the utmost violence. These Central Committees had all been elected in the middle of the summer, or even before, when the Mensheviki and Socialist Revolutionaries had an enormous following; and they delayed or prevented any new elections. Thus, according to the constitution of the Soviets of Workers' and Soldiers' Deputies, the All-Russian Congress *should have been called in September,* but the *Tsay-ee-kah** would not call the meeting, on the ground that the Constituent Assembly was only two months away, at which time, they hinted, the Soviets would abdicate. Meanwhile, one by one, the Bolsheviki were winning in the local Soviets all over the country, in the Union branches and the ranks of the soldiers and sailors. The Peasants' Soviets remained still conservative, because in the sluggish rural districts political consciousness developed slowly, and the Socialist Revolutionary party had been for a generation the party which had agitated among the peasants. . . . But even among the peasants a revolutionary wing was forming. It showed itself clearly in October, when the left wing of the Socialist Revolutionaries split off, and formed a new political faction, the Left Socialist Revolutionaries.

At the same time there were signs everywhere that the forces of reaction were gaining confidence. At the Troitsky Farce theatre in Petrograd, for example, a burlesque called *Sins of the Tsar* was interrupted by a group of Monarchists, who threatened to lynch the

* See Notes and Explanations.

actors for "insulting the Emperor." Certain newspapers began to sigh for a "Russian Napoleon." It was the usual thing among bourgeois *inteligentzia* to refer to the Soviets of Workers' Deputies (Rabotchikh Deputatov) as—Dogs' Deputies.

On October 15th I had a conversation with a great Russian capitalist, Stepan Georgevitch Lianozov, known as the "Russian Rockefeller"—a Cadet by political faith.

"Revolution," he said, "is a sickness. Sooner or later the foreign powers must intervene here—as one would intervene to cure a sick child, and teach it how to walk. Of course it would be more or less improper, but the nations must realise the danger of Bolshevism in their own countries—such contagious ideas as 'proletarian dictatorship,' and 'world social revolution' . . . . There is a chance that this intervention may not be necessary. Transportation is demoralised, the factories are closing down, and the Germans are advancing. Starvation and defeat may bring the Russian people to their senses. . . . "

Mr. Lianozov was emphatic in his opinion that whatever happened, it would be impossible for merchants and manufacturers to permit the existence of the workers' Shop Committees, or to allow the workers any share in the management of industry.

"As for the Bolsheviki, they will be done away with by one of two methods. The Government can evacuate Petrograd, then a state of siege declared, and the military commander of the district can deal with these gentlemen without legal formalities. . . . *Or if, for example, the Constituent Assembly manifests any Utopian tendencies, it cam be dispersed by force of arms. . . . "*

Winter was coming on—the terrible Russian winter. I heard business men speak of it so: "Winter was always Russia's best friend. Perhaps now it will rid us of Revolution." On the freezing front miserable armies continued to starve and die, without enthusiasm. The railways were breaking down, food lessening, factories closing. The desperate masses cried out that the bourgeoisie was sabotaging the life of the people, causing defeat on the Front. Riga had been surrendered just after General Kornilov said publicly, "Must we pay with Riga the price of bringing the country to a sense of its duty?""[*]

To Americans it is incredible that the class war should develop to such a pitch. But I have personally met officers on the Northern Front

* See "Kornilov to Brest-Litovsk," by John Reed. Boni and Liveright. N. Y., 1919.

who frankly preferred military disaster to cooperation with the Soldiers' Committees. The secretary of the Petrograd branch of the Cadet party told me that the break-down of the country's economic life was part of a campaign to discredit the Revolution. An Allied diplomat, whose name I promised not to mention, confirmed this from his own knowledge. I know of certain coal-mines near Kharkov which were fired and flooded by their owners, of textile factories at Moscow whose engineers put the machinery out of order when they left, of railroad officials caught by the workers in the act of crippling locomotives. . . .

A large section of the propertied classes preferred the Germans to the Revolution—even to the Provisional Government—and didn't hesitate to say so. In the Russian household where I lived, the subject of conversation at the dinner-table was almost invariably the coming of the Germans, bringing "law and order." . . . One evening I spent at the house of a Moscow merchant; during tea we asked the eleven people at the table whether they preferred "Wilhelm or the Bolsheviki." The vote was ten to one for Wilhelm. . . .

The speculators took advantage of the universal disorganisation to pile up fortunes, and to spend them in fantastic revelry or the corruption of Government officials. Foodstuffs and fuel were hoarded, or secretly sent out of the country to Sweden. In the first four months of the Revolution, for example, the reserve food-supplies were almost openly looted from the great Municipal warehouses of Petrograd, until the two-years' provision of grain had fallen to less than enough to feed the city for one month. . . . According to the official report of the last Minister of Supplies in the Provisional Government, coffee was bought wholesale in Vladivostok for two rubles a pound, and the consumer in Petrograd paid thirteen. In all the stores of the large cities were tons of food and clothing; but only the rich could buy them.

In a provincial town I knew a merchant family turned speculator — *maradior* (bandit, ghoul) the Russians call it. The three sons had bribed their way out of military service. One gambled in foodstuffs. Another sold illegal gold from the Lena mines to mysterious parties in Finland. The third owned a controlling interest in a chocolate factory, which supplied the local Cooperative societies—on condition that the Cooperatives furnished him everything he needed. And so, while the masses of the people got a quarter pound of black bread on their bread cards, he had an abundance of white bread, sugar, tea, candy, cake and butter. . . . Yet when the soldiers at the front could no longer fight from cold, hunger and exhaustion, how indignantly did this family scream "Cowards !"—how "ashamed" they were "to be Russians" . . . When finally the Bolsheviki found and requisitioned vast hoarded stores of provisions, what "Robbers" they were.

Beneath all this external rottenness moved the old-time Dark Forces, unchanged since the fall of Nicholas the Second, secret still and very active. The agents of the notorious *Okhrana* still functioned, for and against the Tsar, for and against Kerensky—whoever would pay. . . . In the darkness, underground organisations of all sorts, such as the Black Hundreds, were busy attempting to restore reaction in some form or other.

In this atmosphere of corruption, of monstrous half-truths, one clear note sounded day after day, the deepening chorus of the Bolsheviki, "All Power to the Soviets! All power to the direct representatives of millions on millions of common workers, soldiers, peasants. Land, bread, an end to the senseless war, an end to secret diplomacy, speculation, treachery. . . . The Revolution is in danger, and with it the cause of the people all over the world!"

The struggle between the proletariat and the middle class, between the Soviets and the Government, which had begun in the first March days, was about to culminate. Having at one bound leaped from the Middle Ages into the twentieth century, Russia showed the startled world two systems of Revolution—the political and the socia—in mortal combat.

What a revelation of the vitality of the Russian Revolution, after all these months of starvation and disillusionment! The bourgeoisie should have better known its Russia. Not for a long time in Russia will the "sickness" of Revolution have run its course. . . .

Discussion Questions

1. Why were the Bolsheviks successful in assuming the leadership of the peasants, soldiers, and workers who provided the momentum for the revolution?

2. How does Reed explain class war to his American audience?

Sources

John Reed, *Ten Days that Shook the World*, New York: International Publishers, 1926.

Robert A. Rosenstone, *Romantic Revolutionary: A Biography of John Reed*, New York: Vintage Books, 1975.

ERICH MARIA REMARQUE, *ALL QUIET ON THE WESTERN FRONT*

Erich Maria Remarque was born in northern Germany in 1898. After completing his schooling at a Catholic institution, Remarque entered a teaching school in 1916. His studies there were interrupted by the outbreak of World War I. Called up for service that November and sent to the front in July, Remarque suffered a splinter wound during the Flanders offensive of the British. During his recovery, his mother died. When the war ended, Remarque finished his teacher training and then drifted from job to job during the chaos of Weimar Germany in the 1920s. He honed his writing skills in advertising before obtaining an editorship at a magazine. He published *All Quiet on the Western Front* in 1929 after several publishers hesitated to put the novel to press. The Nazis accused him of betraying his German comrades when they came to power in 1933. Remarque went into exile, first in Switzerland. He emigrated to the United States on the eve of World War II with the help of his friend Marlene Dietrich. Remarque became a popular figure among European exiles, living in Hollywood and New York. When his sister was executed by the Nazis in 1943, Remarque resigned himself to remaining outside of Germany. He applied for U.S. citizenship in 1947, but returned to Switzerland a year later, where he lived for most of the remainder of his life. He continued to write, penning a dozen novels, most of which dealt with the issued raised by the wars that convulsed the European continent in the first half of the twentieth century.

All Quiet on the Western Front explores the experiences of a young soldier named Paul during World War I. Sent to the trenches, Paul represents the millions of young soldiers who died during the conflict. Critics on both the right and the left attacked Remarque, but the book won over the reading public in Germany and internationally. In the excerpt that follows, he kills a man at close quarters for the first time. The enemy soldier lingers in agony, forcing Paul to confront the senselessness of the war.

ALL QUIET ON THE WESTERN FRONT

Erich Maria Remarque

Instead of going to Russia we go up the line again. On the way we pass through what is left of a wood, with half-blasted tree-trunks and the ground looking as if it had been ploughed up. There are some massive craters. 'Christ, this place took a pounding,' I say to Kat.

'Mortar fire,' he replies, and then points upwards.

Dead men are hanging in the trees. In one of them a naked soldier is squatting in the branches; his helmet is still on his head, but otherwise he has nothing on. There is only the top half of him up there, a head and body with the legs missing.

'What happened there?' I ask.

'Blown out of his uniform,' grunts Tjaden.

'It's funny,' says Kat, 'but we've seen that a few times. When a trench mortar goes off you actually do get blown out of your clothes. It's the blast that does it.'

I look around. It really is true. In some trees there are just bits of uniform, others have a bit of bloody pulp that was once a human limb sticking to them. There is one body which only has a scrap of underpants on one leg and the tunic collar around the neck. Otherwise it is naked. The uniform is hanging in the nearby trees. Both arms are missing from the body, as if they have been wrenched out of their sockets. I come across one of them in the undergrowth twenty paces away.

The dead man is lying on his face. The earth is black from the blood underneath the arm sockets. The ground is scuffed by his feet, as though he went on kicking for a while.

'It's no joke, Kat,' I say.

'Nor is a bit of shrapnel in the guts,' he says with a shrug.

'The main thing is not to let it all get to you,' adds Tjaden.

All this can't have happened too long ago, because the blood is still fresh. Since all the soldiers we find are dead we don't hang about there, but just report the business at the next dressing station. After all, there's no reason why we should do the donkey work for the stretcher-bearers.

*   *   *

A patrol has to be sent out to establish how many of the enemy positions are still manned. Because I've had leave, I still feel a bit awkward as far as the others are concerned, and for that reason I volunteer to join it. We agree on a plan of action; crawl through the wire, and then separate, so that we can move forward independently. After a while I find a shallow crater and slip into it. I take a look at things from there.

The area is being covered by moderate machine-gun fire. They are sweeping it from all sides, and the fire is not very heavy, but still enough for you to make sure you keep your head well down.

A Verey light goes up. The terrain looks barren in the pale glow. By contrast, it seems so much darker when the night closes in again. They told us back in the trenches that there are supposed to be black soldiers in the opposite trenches. That's bad, because they are hard to see, and besides, they are very good at reconnaissance patrols. Curiously enough, they can often be just plain careless. Both Kat and Kropp have been on patrols where they have shot black soldiers out on counter-reconnaissance who were so keen on cigarettes that they were smoking as they moved along. All Kat and Albert had to do was to get a glowing tip in their sights and aim at that.

A small shell whistles down and strikes close to where I am. I hadn't heard it coming and it gives me a real fright. At that moment I'm overcome by mindless panic. I'm out here on my own in the dark and wellnigh helpless—for all I know two eyes have already been watching me for ages from another shell hole and there is a hand-grenade just waiting to blow me to bits. I try to pull myself together. This isn't my first patrol and it isn't even a particularly dangerous one. But it is the first one I've been on since I was on leave, and on top of that the terrain is still pretty unfamiliar to me.

I tell myself firmly that I am getting worked up for nothing, that there is probably no one watching for me in the dark because if there were they wouldn't be firing so low.

It's no use. Thoughts buzz round in my head in complete confusion —I hear my mother's warning voice, I see the Russians leaning against the wire-netting, with their beards blowing in the wind, I get a bright and wonderful picture of a canteen with comfortable chairs, then of a cinema in Valenciennes, and then, horrible in my tortured imagination, of a gun barrel, grey and unfeeling, following me around silently wherever I try to turn my head: sweat is breaking out from every pore.

I am still lying in the hollow I found. I look at my watch; only a few minutes have passed. My forehead is wet, there is dampness all round my eyes, my hands are shaking and I'm coughing quietly. It's nothing more than a bad attack of fear, of common-or-garden cold terror at the prospect of sticking my head out and crawling on.

All my tense readiness melts into the desire to stay lying down. My limbs are glued to the ground, I try to move, but I can't—they just won't come away from it. I press myself into the earth, I cannot move forwards, and I decide to stay where I am.

But right away a new wave comes over me, a wave of shame, of regret, and yet still one of self-preservation. I lift myself up slightly to have a look around. My eyes are stinging and I stare into the darkness. Then a Verey light goes up and I duck down again.

I am fighting a crazy, confused battle. I want to get out of my hollow in the ground and I keep on slipping back in; I say to myself, 'You've got to, it's to do with your mates, not some stupid order,' and straight after that: 'So what? I've only got the one life to lose.'

*   *   *

It's all because of that leave, I tell myself bitterly by way of an excuse. But I don't believe it myself, I just feel horribly drained. I raise myself up slowly and stretch out my arms, then raise my back and prop myself half on the edge of the shell hole.

Then I hear sounds and get down again. In spite of the thunder of the guns you can pick out suspicious noises completely clearly. I listen—the sound is coming from behind me. It is our soldiers moving through the trench. Now I can even hear muted voices. From the sound of it it might even be Kat speaking.

Suddenly a surprising warmth comes over me. Those voices, those few soft words, those footsteps in the trench behind me tear me with a jolt away from the terrible feeling of isolation that goes with the fear of death, to which I nearly succumbed. Those voices mean more than my life, more than mothering and fear, they are the strongest and most protective thing that there is: they are the voices of my pals.

I'm no longer a shivering scrap of humanity alone in the dark—I belong to them and they to me, we all share the same fear and the same life, and we are bound to each other in a strong and simple way. I want to press my face into them, those voices, those few words that saved me, and which will be my support.

*   *   *

I slip warily over the edge, and snake forwards. I creep along on all fours; things are going well, I fix the direction, look about me and take note of the pattern of artillery fire so that I can find my way back. Then I try to make contact with the others.

I am still afraid, but now it is a rational fear, which is just an extraordinarily enhanced cautiousness. It is a windy night, and the shadows move back and forth in the sudden flashes from the gunfire. By this light you can see too much and too little. Often I freeze suddenly, but there is never anything there. In this way I get quite a long distance forward, and then turn back in a curve. I haven't made contact. Every few feet closer to our trench makes me more confident, but I still move as fast as I can. It wouldn't be too good to stop one just at this moment.

And then I get another shock. I'm no longer able to make out the exact direction. Silently I crouch in a shell hole and try and get my bearings. It has happened more than once that a man has jumped cheerfully into a trench, and only then found out that it was the wrong side.

After a while I listen again. I still haven't sorted out where I am. The wilderness of shell holes seems so confusing that in my agitated state I no longer have any idea which way to go. Maybe I am crawling parallel with the trenches, and I could go on for ever doing that. So I make another turn.

These damned Verey lights! It feels as if they last for an hour, and you can't make a move, or things soon start whistling round you.

It's no use, I've got to get out. By fits and starts I work my way along. I crawl crabwise across the ground and tear my hands to pieces on ragged bits of shrapnel as sharp as razor-blades. Often I get the impression that the sky is becoming lighter on the horizon, but that could just be my imagination. Gradually I realize that I am crawling for my life.

A shell hits. Then straight away two more. And then it really starts. A barrage. Machine-guns chatter. Now there is nothing in the world that

I can do except lie low. It seems to be an offensive. Light-rockets go up everywhere. Incessantly.

I'm lying bent double in a big shell hole in water up to my waist. When the offensive starts I'll drop into the water as far as I can without drowning and put my face in the mud. I'll have to play dead.

Suddenly I hear their shellfire give way. Straight away I slip down into the water at the bottom of the shell hole, my helmet right on the back of my neck and my mouth only sufficiently above water to let me breathe.

Then I remain motionless—because somewhere there is a clinking noise, something is coming closer, moving along and stamping; every nerve in my body tenses up and freezes. The clinking noise moves on over me, the first wave of soldiers is past. All that I had in my head was the one explosive thought: what will you do if someone jumps into your shell hole? Now I quickly pull out my small dagger, grip it tight and hide it by keeping my hand downwards in the mud. The idea keeps pounding in my brain that if anyone jumps in I'll stab him immediately, stick the knife into his throat at once, so that he can't shout out, there's no other way, he'll be as frightened as I am, and we'll attack each other purely out of fear, so I have to get there first.

Now our gun batteries are firing. There is an impact near me. That makes me furiously angry, that's all I need, to be hit by our own gunfire; I curse into the mud and grind my teeth, it's an outburst of rage, and in the end all I can do is groan and plead.

The crash of shells pounds against my ears. If our men launch a counter-offensive, I'm free. I press my head against the earth and I can hear the dull thunder like distant explosions in a mine—then I lift my head to listen to the noises above me.

The machine-guns are rattling away. I know that our barbed-wire entanglements are firm and pretty well undamaged; sections of them are electrified. The gunfire increases. They aren't getting through. They'll have to turn back.

I collapse into the shell hole again, tense almost to breaking point. Clattering, crawling, clinking—it all becomes audible, a single scream ringing out in the midst of it all. They're coming under fire, the attack has been held off.

*   *   *

It's got a little bit lighter. Footsteps hurry by me. The first few. Past me. Then some more. The rattle of the machine-guns becomes continuous. I am just about to turn round a bit when suddenly there is a noise and a body falls on to me in the shell hole, heavily and with a splash, then slips and lands on top of me—

I don't think at all, I make no decision—I just stab wildly and feel only how the body jerks, then goes limp and collapses. When I come to myself again, my hand is sticky and wet.

The other man makes a gurgling noise. To me it sounds as if he is roaring, every breath is like a scream, like thunder—but it is only the blood in my own veins that is pounding so hard. I'd like to stop his mouth, to stuff earth into it, to stab again—he has to be quiet or he'll give me away; but I am so much myself again and suddenly feel so weak that I can't raise my hand against him any more.

So I crawl away into the furthest corner and stay there, my eyes fixed on him, gripping my knife, ready to go for him again if he moves—but he won't do anything again. I can hear that just from his gurgling.

I can only see him indistinctly. I have the one single desire—to get away. If I don't do so quickly it will be too light; it's already difficult. But the moment I try to raise my head I become aware that it is impossible. The machine-gun fire is so dense that I would be full of holes before I had gone a step.

I have another go, lifting up my helmet and pushing it forwards to gauge the height of fire. A moment later a bullet knocks it out of my hand. The gunfire is sweeping the ground at a very low level. I am not far enough away from the enemy trenches to escape being hit by one of the snipers the moment I tried to make a break for it.

It gets lighter and lighter. I wait desperately for an attack by our men. My knuckles are white because I am tensing my hands, praying for the firing to die down and for my mates to come.

The minutes trickle past one by one. I daren't look at the dark figure in the shell hole any more. With great effort I look past him, and wait, just wait. The bullets hiss, they are a mesh of steel, it won't stop, it won't stop.

Then I see my bloodied hand and suddenly I feel sick. I take some earth and rub it on to the skin, now at least my hand is dirty and you can't see the blood any more.

The gunfire still doesn't die down. It's just as strong now from both sides. Our lot have probably long since given me up for lost.

* * *

It is a light, grey, early morning. The gurgling still continues. I block my ears, but I quickly have to take my hands away from them because otherwise I won't be able to hear anything else.

The figure opposite me moves. That startles me, and I look across at him, although I don't want to. Now my eyes are riveted on him. A man with a little moustache is lying there, his head hanging lopsidedly, one arm half crooked and the head against it. The other hand is clasped to his chest. It has blood on it.

He's dead, I tell myself, he must be dead, he can't feel anything any more; that gurgling, it can only be the body. But the head tries to lift itself and for a moment the groaning gets louder, the forehead sinks back on to the arm. The man is not dead. He is dying, but he is not dead. I push myself forward, pause, prop myself on my hands, slip a bit further along, wait—further, a terrible journey of three yards, a long and fearsome journey. At last I am by his side.

Then he opens his eyes. He must have been able to hear me and he looks at me with an expression of absolute terror. His body doesn't move, but in his eyes there is such an incredible desire to get away that I can imagine for a moment that they might summon up enough strength to drag his body with them, carrying him hundreds of miles away, far, far away, at a single leap. The body is still, completely quiet, there is not a single sound, and even the gurgling has stopped, but the eyes are screaming, roaring, all his life has gathered in them and formed itself into an incredible urge to escape, into a terrible fear of death, a fear of me.

My legs give way and I fall down on to my elbows. 'No, no,' I whisper.

The eyes follow me. I am quite incapable of making any movement as long as they are watching me.

Then his hand falls slowly away from his chest, just a little way, dropping only an inch or two. But that movement breaks the spell of the eyes. I lean forward, shake my head and whisper, 'No, no, no' and lift up my hand—I have to show him that I want to help him, and I wipe his forehead.

The eyes flinched when my hand came close, but now they lose their fixed gaze, the eyelids sink deeper, the tension eases. I open his collar for him and prop his head a bit more comfortably.

His mouth is half open and he makes an attempt to form some words. His lips are dry. I haven't got my water bottle, I didn't bring it with me. But there is water in the mud at the bottom of the shell hole. I scramble down, take out my handkerchief, spread it out, press it down, then cup my hand and scoop up the yellow water that seeps through it.

He swallows it. I fetch more. Then I unbutton his tunic so that I can bandage his wounds, if I can. I have to do that anyway, so that if I get caught the other lot can see that I tried to help him, and won't shoot me outright. He tries to push me away, but his hand is too weak. The shirt is stuck fast and I can't move it aside, and since it is buttoned at the back there is nothing for it but to slit it open.

I look for my knife and find it again. But as soon as I start to cut the shirt open his eyes open wide again and that scream is in them once more, and the look of panic, so that I have to close them, press them shut and whisper, 'I'm trying to help you, comrade, *camarade, camarade, camarade,*—' and I stress the word so that he understands me.

There are three stab wounds. My pack of field dressings covers them but the blood flows out underneath, so I press them down more firmly, and he groans.

It's all I can do. Now we must just wait, wait.

*   *   *

Hours. The gurgling starts up again—how long it takes for a man to die! What I do know is that he is beyond saving. To be sure, I have tried to convince myself otherwise, but by midday this self-delusion has melted away, has been shot to pieces by his groans. If I hadn't lost my revolver when I was crawling along I would shoot him. I can't stab him.

By midday I am in that twilight area where reason evaporates. I am ravenously hungry, almost weeping for want of food, but I can't help it. I fetch water several times for the dying man and I drink some of it myself.

This is the first man I have ever killed with my own hands, the first one I've seen at close quarters whose death I've caused. Kat and Kropp and Müller have all seen people they have hit as well, it happens often, it's quite common in hand-to-hand fighting—

But every gasp strips my heart bare. The dying man is the master of these hours, he has an invisible dagger to stab me with: the dagger of time and my own thoughts.

I would give a lot for him to live. It is hard to lie here and have to watch and listen to him.

By three in the afternoon he is dead.

I breathe again. But only for a short time. Soon the silence seems harder for me to bear than the groans. I would even like to hear the gurgling again; in fits and starts, hoarse, sometimes a soft whistling noise and then hoarse and loud again.

*   *   *

What I am doing is crazy. But I have to have something to do. So I move the dead man again so that he is lying more comfortably, even though he can't feel anything any more. I close his eyes. They are brown. His hair is black and slightly curly at the sides. His mouth is full and soft underneath his moustache; his nose is a little angular and his skin is tanned—it doesn't seem as pale as before, when he was still alive. For a moment his face even manages to look almost healthy, and then it gives way quickly to become the face of a dead stranger, one of the many I have seen, and every one of them looks alike.

His wife is bound to be thinking of him just now: she doesn't know what has happened. He looks as if he used to write to her a lot; she will go on getting his letters, too -tomorrow, next week— maybe a stray one in a month's time. She'll read it, and he'll be speaking to her in it.

My state of mind is getting worse all the time, and I can't control my thoughts. What does his wife look like? Like the slim dark girl in the house by the canal? Doesn't she belong to me? Perhaps she belongs to me now because of all this! If only Kantorek were sitting here by me! What if my mother saw me in this state—The dead man would surely have been able to live for another thirty years if I'd taken more care about how I was going to get back. If only he had been running a couple of yards further to the left he'd be back in his trench over there writing another letter to his wife.

But this will get me nowhere, it's the fate we all share. If Kemmerich's leg had been a few inches further to the right, if Haie had leaned an inch or two further forward—

Discussion Questions

1. Why do you think the Nazis viewed Remarque as a traitor for writing *All Quiet on the Western Front?*
2. Does Remarque find anything redeeming in the experience of war?

Sources

Erich Maria Remarque, *All Quiet on the Western Front*, trans. Brian Murdoch, London: Jonathon Cape, 1994.

Richard Arthur Firda, *All Quiet on the Western Front: Literary Analysis and Cultural Context*, New York: Twayne Publishers, 1993.

CHAPTER 23

Anna Akhmatova
Selected Poems

Adolph Hitler
Perish the Jew

ANNA AKHMATOVA, SELECTED POEMS

In 1889, Anna Akhmatova was born on the coast of the Black Sea, the daughter of a marine engineer . Although she spent her childhood outside of Petersburg and later in the north, her family always returned to the sea in the summer, much to Akhmatova's joy. She first heard poetry from her mother before she could read, and she wrote her first poem at the age of eleven. She married in 1910, and the newlyweds traveled to Paris, where Akhmatova, with a group of young poets, founded a new literary movement, Acmeism. Her first volume of poetry, published in 1912, won her instant recognition. She bore a son that same year. World War I set off the changes that would soon touch Akhmatova's family and friends.

In the aftermath of the Russian revolution, Akhmatova witnessed the imprisonment, death, and exile of her loved ones. Her only defense against these abuses were the words of her poems. Her marriage failed, and her ex-husband was shot in 1921. Her son was arrested repeatedly, as was her second husband. Some friends survived the labor camps; others succumbed to the hardship. Akhmatova herself was not directly persecuted, but the Communist party refused to publish her poems in the 1920s and '30s. A series of poems written in response to the Russian experience during World War II redeemed her in the eyes of the party. She and other writers were evacuated during the siege of Leningrad in 1941. At the close of the war, she was again censored. Near the end of her life, she witnessed the painful process of coming to terms with the government's repressive measures in the preceding decades. By the time of her death in 1966, she had been recognized and honored by admirers and critics at home and abroad.

Always painfully aware of the historical events that touched her life on such a personal level, Akhmatova wielded a rare gift for conveying the feelings of very specific moments and events through her poetry. The following poems, taken from the "Wind of War" cycle written during World War II, lament the losses sustained by Russian on the eastern front of the war.

SELECTED POEMS

Anna Akhmatova

THE WIND OF WAR

1

VOW

And she who is parting with her sweetheart today –
Let her forge her pain into strength.
By the children we swear, we swear by the graves,
That no one will force us to submit!

July 1941
Leningrad

2

Grandly they said good-bye to the girls,
Nonchalantly kissed Mother,
All dressed in brand-new clothes,
As if they were going to play soldier.

No bad, no good, no in-between . . .
They all took their place,
Where there is neither first, nor last . . .

They all lay down to sleep.

1943

3

FIRST LONG-RANGE FIRING ON LENINGRAD

And people's colorful daily round
Suddenly changed drastically.
But this was not a city sound,
Nor one heard in the villages.
It resembled a distant peal of thunder
As closely as one brother resembles another,
But in thunder there's the moisture
Of cool cloud towers
And the yearning of the meadows—
For the news of joyous showers.
But this was like scorching heat, dry,
And we didn't want to believe
The rumor we heard-because of
How it grew and multiplied,
Because of how indifferently
It brought death to my child.

September 1941

4

The birds of death are at the zenith.
Who will rescue Leningrad?

Be quiet—it is breathing,
It's still living, it hears everything:

How at the bottom of the Baltic Sea
Its sons groan in their sleep,

How from its depths come cries: "Bread!"
That reach to the firmament . . .

But this solid earth is pitiless.
And staring from all the windows—death.

September 28, 1941
(On the airplane)

5

COURAGE

We know what lies in balance at this moment,
And what is happening right now.
The hour for courage strikes upon our clocks,
And courage will not desert us.
We're not frightened by a hail of lead,
We're not bitter without a roof overhead—
And we will preserve you, Russian speech,
Mighty Russian word!
We will transmit you to our grandchildren
Free and pure and rescued from captivity
Forever!

February 23, 1942
Tashkent

6

Trenches have been dug in the garden,
No lights shine.
Peter's orphans,
Oh, my children!
It's hard to breathe underground,
Your temples throb,
Through the bombardment is heard
The voice of a child.

7

Knock with your little fist—I will open.
I always opened the door to you.
I am beyond the high mountain now,
Beyond the desert, beyond the wind and the heat,
But I will never abandon you . . .
I didn't hear your groans,
You never asked me for bread.
Bring me a twig from the maple tree

Or simply a little green grass,
As you did last spring.
Bring me in your cupped palms
Some of our cool, pure, Neva water,
And I will wash the bloody traces
From your golden hair.

April 23, 1942
Tashkent

8

NOX

The statue "Night" in the Summer Garden

Little night!
Draped in stars,
In funereal poppies, with a sleepless owl . . .
Little daughter!
We hid you under
The garden's fresh dirt.
Empty now are the cups of Dionysus,
The gazes of love are stained with tears . . .
Passing over our city are
Your terrible sisters.

May 30, 1942

9

TO THE VICTORS

The Narvsky Gates were behind,
Ahead there was only death . . .
Thus the Soviet infantry marched
Straight into Big Bertha's blazing barrels.
They will write books about you:
"You laid down your life for your friends,"
Unpretentious lads—

Vankas, Vaskas, Alyoshkas, Grislikas—
Grandsons, brothers, sons!

February 29, 1944
Tashkent

10

And you, my friends from the latest call-up!
My life has been spared to mourn for you.
Not to freeze over your memory as a weeping willow,
But to shout all your names to the whole wide world!
But never mind names!
None of that matters—You are with us!
Everyone down on your knees!
A crimson light pours!
And the Leningraders come through the smoke in
even rows—
The living and the dead: for glory never dies.

August 1942
Dyurmen

11

To the right the vacant lots unfurl,
There's a strip of dawn as ancient as the world.

To the left, streetlights like gallows trees,
One, two, three . . .

And over everything a jackdaw's cry
And the moon's pallid face
Arise completely irrelevantly.

It's—not from this life and not from that one,
It's—when the golden age will dawn,

It's—when the war is over,
It's—when we meet once more.

April 29, 1944
Tashkent

VICTORY

1(12)

Something glorious is beginning gloriously,
With a thunderous crash, in snowy clouds,
Where the immaculate body of the land languishes,
Defiled by the enemy.
From there our native birches are stretching out their
branches
To us, and waiting, and calling out to us,
And mighty Father Frosts
Are marching in formation with us.

January 1942

Discussion Questions

1. How does Akhmatova portray Russian experiences of World War II?

2. Why do you think this series of poems restored Akhmatova's good standing with the Communist party?

Sources

Judith Hemschemeyer, trans. *The Compete Poems of Anna Akhmatova,* Vol. II, Somerville: Zephyr Press, 1990.

Konstantin Polivanov, *Anna Akhmatova and Her Circle,* trans. Patricia Beriozkina, Fayetteville: University of Arkansas Press, 1994.

ADOLF HITLER,
PERISH THE JEW

Adolf Hitler's meteoric rise to power belied his mediocre beginnings. Born to a comfortable family in Austria Hungary in 1889, Hitler performed poorly in school. He entertained notions of becoming an artist, but was rejected by the Vienna Academy of Fine Arts. Both of his parents had died by 1908, and Hitler promptly wasted his inheritance. After a short spell in a homeless shelter, he eked out a living painting postcards. When World War I broke out, Hitler volunteered and remained in service for the duration of the war. Hitler had already formed many of the political ideas that would inform his dictatorial reign over Germany by the time he joined the army. His rampant anti-Semitism had already taken root, and at the end of the war, he vowed to redeem Germany from their grasp.

Hitler was immediately attracted to the National Socialist German Workers Party, or the Nazis. His oratory talents catapulted him to the leadership of the party by the summer of 1921. In his speeches, Hitler played upon the fears and frustrations of his German audience. The burden of reparations payments created an economic crisis of disastrous proportions by 1923. Prematurely, Hitler and several hundred of his Nazi disciples attempted a coup. They were defeated, and Hitler was imprisoned. He used the notoriety he gained from the failed coup, also known as the beer hall putsch, to increase his following. He also used his time in prison to draft *Mein Kampf*, a work that outlined his political philosophy. Once released in 1924, Hitler worked doggedly to expand the Nazi party. In his first election in 1928, he won a mere three percent of the vote. But the Depression aided his cause, and by 1932, the Nazis held the majority in the Reichstag. Hitler then forced President Hindenburg to appoint him chancellor, and swiftly acted to secure his power. As he secured his control over Germany, Hitler began to implement his political philosophy in practical ways. The first laws limiting the rights of Jews were enacted in 1933. The first concentration camps received Jews by 1938. At the same time, Hitler rearmed Germany in anticipation of his expansionist moves toward the end of the decade. His aggression triggered World War II, and his policies resulted in the deliberate extermination of millions of people.

In the speeches below, delivered in 1922 shortly after Hitler had joined the Nazi party, he explains the foundations for his anti-Semitism. He blames the Jews for a number of social problems, and points to the dangers that they pose politically to the German state. Few could imagine, a decade before he first seized power, the tragic consequences of his racially-motivated hatred.

PERISH THE JEW

Adolph Hitler

IN BEHALF OF CHRIST

Did the Jew have an interest in the collapse [of 1918]? Today we can discuss that objectively. You probably know that comparatively speaking very few Jews have suffered. Let no one say to me: The poor Eastern Jew! Naturally they did not have anything to begin with, for the simple reason that they came from a country which they had pillaged and eaten to the bone for centuries, and have never been and never will be productively active.

It is quite logical that these gentlemen arrived poor to begin with. But just look at such an Oriental after he has been here for five or six years. Compare the million workers in Berlin in 1914 with what they are today. . . . How have they changed? They have gotten thinner; their clothes are ragged and worn; they have become poor. And now go look for the 100,000 Eastern Jews who immigrated during the first years of the war. You will not find them today. Most of them have made good and already own automobiles. This has come about not because the Jews are more clever—for I defy you to say that the decent and honest working people are nothing but blockheads. The sole reason is that these 100,000 Jews were never ready to work along honorably in a national organism for the common good. From the very beginning, they regarded this entire national organism as nothing more than a hot-house for them to thrive in.

The Jew has not become poorer. He is slowly bloating up, and if you do not believe this, I beg you to go and look in our health resorts. There you will find two kinds of people: The German, who goes there to catch a breath of fresh air for the first time in a long while and to get rested; and the Jew, who goes there to get rid of his fat. If you go out into our mountains, whom do you find in new yellow boots, with beautiful knapsacks, the contents of which generally do not amount to much anyway? And why should they? The Jews go up to the hotel, generally as far as the train goes, and where the train stops there they also stop. They sit around within a kilometer's distance of the hotel, like blowflies around a cadaver.

These are certainly not our "working" classes—neither our intellectual nor our physical workers. You generally find the "working" classes in worn clothing, climbing about somewhere off to the side, for the simple reason that they feel ashamed even to enter this perfumed atmosphere with their old-fashioned clothes dating from 1913 and 1914. The Oberammergan Passion Plays this summer will show you just who has the time, the leisure, and the money to enjoy nature and the spectacle of Christ's sufferings. No, the Jew certainly did not suffer privations. . . .

The same Jew, who as a majority Socialist or as an Independent led you in those days [November 1918], still leads you. No matter whether he is an Independent or a Communist, he has remained the same. And just as he did not look after your interests at that time but after the interests of the capital of his own race, so today he certainly will not lead you in the fight against his race and its capital. On the contrary, he will prevent you from fighting your real exploiters. He will never help to liberate you, for he is not the one who is enslaved.

While now in Soviet Russia millions are starving and dying, while in Soviet Russia 30,000,000 so-called "Proletarians" lie prostrate, clawing roots and grass from the soil in order to prolong their lives for even a few days or weeks, Chicherin and a delegation of about 200 Soviet Jews are traveling through Europe on special trains, going to night clubs, attending strip-teases, and living in the best of hotels. As a matter of fact they are better off than the millions of so-called "Bourgeois" you once thought you had to fight. The 400 Soviet comissars of Jewish nationality are not suffering want, nor the thousands upon thousands of deputy comissars. On the contrary. All the treasures which the "Proletarian" in his madness took from the so-called "Bourgeoisie" in order to fight so-called capitalism, have all now gotten into the hands of the Soviet comissars. It is true that a few workers in those days took the pocketbook of his landlord or his employer; it is true that he took rings and diamonds and rejoiced at being in possession of the treasures formerly owned only by the "Bourgeoisie." But in his hands those possessions are dead, yes, really dead gold. They do not do him any good. He is stuck in his wilderness and he cannot feed himself on diamonds. He gives millions in value for a crust of bread. But the bread is in the hands of the State Central Organization and that is in the hands of the Jews. In, that way everything, absolutely everything, that the common man once thought he was winning for himself, flows right back into the hands of his seducers.

The Jew accomplished it. A redistribution of wealth took place, but not according to the desire of the masses. It was nothing more than a shifting of wealth. Millions of men were deprived of their last ruble, which they had once saved honestly, honorably, and carefully. These rubles, by the millions, now became the property of those who as leaders had not done anything and who are not doing anything today except to starve and bleed the people. And now, my dear *Volksgenossen*, do you believe that those people who are doing the same thing here will end the Revolution [of 1918]? They do not wish to end the Revolution for there is no necessity for them to do so. The Revolution is for them nothing but milk and honey and furthermore they cannot end the Revolution..

The Aryan regards work as the basis for the maintenance of the national community as such; the Jew regards work as a means of exploiting other peoples. The Jew never works as a productive creator without the great prospect of becoming the master. He works unproductively, using and profiting from the work of others. We therefore understand the iron words once pronounced by Mommsen: The Jew is the ferment of the decomposition of peoples. This means that the-Jew destroys and has to destroy, because he is completely lacking in any concept of work for the common good. It does not matter whether the individual Jew is "decent" or not. He has certain traits which nature has given him and he can never rid himself of these traits. The Jew is harmful to us. Whether he harms us consciously or unconsciously is not the question. We must consciously protect the welfare of our people. . . .

We were finally the ones who pointed out to the people on a large scale the peril which crept into our midst, a peril which millions of people did not realize, but which will nevertheless lead us all to ruin— the Jewish peril. Today people again say that we are "agitators." In this respect I should like to make reference to someone greater than myself. Count Lerchenfeld declared in the last session of the *Landtag*, that his feeling "as man and as Christian" keeps him from being an anti-Semite. I say: My feeling as a Christian points me to my Lord and Savior as a fighter. It points me to the man who, once lonely and with only a few followers, recognized these Jews for what they were, and called men to fight them, and who, so help me, was greatest not as a sufferer but as a fighter. With boundless love, as a Christian and as a man, I read the passage which relates how the Lord finally gathered His strength and made use of the whip in order to drive the the vipers, and cheats from the temple. Today, 2,000 years later, I recognize with deep emotion Christ's tremendous fight for this world against the Jewish poison. I recognize it most profoundly by the fact that He had to shed His blood on the cross for this fight. As a Christian it is not my duty to permit myself to be cheated but it is my duty to be a champion of truth and of right.

As man it is my duty to see to it that humanity will not suffer the same catastrophic collapse as did an old civilization about 2,000 years ago, a civilization which was also driven to destruction by the Jewish people. In those days, however, when Rome fell, new and endless masses of Germanic peoples poured in from the North to take its place. But if Germany were to fall today, who will follow after us? The Germanic blood on this earth is slowly being exhausted unless we gather up all our strength and free ourselves. . . .

As a Christian I owe something to my own people. I see how this people is working and working, laboring and exerting itself, and still at the end of the week it has nothing but misery and poverty to show for it. One perhaps does not realize it in the homes of the nobility. But when I go out in the mornings and see those people in the bread-lines and look into their drawn faces, then I become convinced that I am a veritable devil and not a Christian if I do not feel compassion and do not wage war, as our Lord did 2,000 years ago, against those who are pillaging and exploiting this poor people.

To be sure, the people is aroused today by this misery. Outwardly it may appear apathetic, but inwardly it is fermenting. Many a person may say that it is an accursed crime to arouse passion under such circumstances. And I tell myself: Passion will be aroused by increasing misery and this passion will manifest itself in one way or another. I therefore ask this question of those who today are calling us "agitators": What do you have to offer the people in the way of a belief to which they may cling? Nothing at all. For you yourself do not believe in your own prescriptions. That is the mightiest mission of our Movement, namely, to give the searching and bewildered masses a new, firm belief, a belief which will not abandon them in these days of chaos, which they will swear and abide by, so that at least somewhere they will again find a place where their hearts can be at rest. We are going to accomplish this! It is proved by the thousands who keep coming to us and who perhaps for the first time in years find something worth living for again. . . .

Two thousand years ago a man was likewise denounced by this particular race which today is denouncing and blaspheming everywhere; by the race which is agitating everywhere and which regards every opposition to it as an accursed crime. That man was dragged into court and they said then: He is arousing the people! So he also was "agitating!" And against whom? Against "God," they cried. Yes indeed, he was agitating against the "god" of the Jews, for that "god" is money (Munich, April 12, 1922; *Voelkiseher Beobachter*, April 22, 1922).

DESTROYER OF CIVILIZATION

The Jew became the founder of the Social Democratic Movement, at that time. He succeeded with exceptional cleverness in securing the leadership more and more by means of two measures. He applied one measure on the Right, the other measure on the Left, for he had his apostles in both camps. As regards the Right, he tried to exaggerate all existing shortcomings to such an extent that through the emphasis on those things which necessarily antagonize the common man, the poor devil, the latter would be aroused as much as possible. It was the Jew who caused the greed for money to increase to an extreme. It was he who finally preached that unscrupulousness in the attainment of business ends was a matter of course. It was he who forced others to use the same methods because of his competition. It was he who became so heartless in the attainment of his ends that the saying, "Business, too, marches over corpses," became generally accepted. It was the Jew in particular whose repulsive insolence aroused the deadly hatred of the great masses. While the Jew on the one hand corrupted people by his bad example, he polluted their blood by systematic bastardization. More and more Jews filtered into the upper families, and it was from the Jews that the latter took their wives. The result was that in a short time it was precisely the leading class of the nation that had become completely estranged from its own people.

This was the prerequisite for the Jew's work on the Left. He made good use of this prerequisite. On the Left he was the common demagogue. Two measures were sufficient for him to drive the national intelligentsia from the leadership of the working class. First, there was the international approach. The Jew knew only too well that the moment he convinced the working class of the necessity of the international approach in his life and struggle, the national intelligentsia would drop out of the working class movement. For it would not continue under such circumstances. The national intelligentsia is willing to make the greatest sacrifices, to do everything for its people, but it cannot be so insane as to believe that a people can be made happy and prosperous by renouncing the existence of that people, by renouncing its own rights, and by abolishing national resistance toward foreign elements. The national intelligentsia could not do that and so it stayed away. Then there was the Jew's second measure—Marxist theory. The moment the statement is made that private property as such is theft, that is, in other words, as soon as one forsakes the self-evident formula that only natural resources can and should be common property, but that everything that anyone earns honestly should be his, from that moment too the economic intelligentsia with national ideals could no longer cooperate, for it realized that this theory would lead to the collapse of all human culture. Thus the Jew succeeded in isolating this new movement [of the workers] from all national elements. Furthermore, the Jew succeeded, by an ingenious exploitation of the press, in influencing the masses to such an extent that the faults of the Left appeared to the Right as the faults of the German worker, and the faults of the Right at the same time appeared to the German worker as the faults of the German middle class. Neither of the two groups realized that the faults of both sides were the result of a scheme, planned by devilish foreign agitators. This alone explains how the greatest farce in history was possible, namely, how the Jews of the stock exchange could become the leaders of the German Workers Movement. It is a gigantic fraud, the like of which is seldom seen in world history. . . .

In all this one can see again and again how well they work together, the Jew from the stock exchange and the leader of the workers; the newspaper of the stock exchange and the organ of the workers . . . While the business agent Moses Cohn persuades his company to react most unfavorably to the demands of the workers, his brother Isaac Cohn, the labor leader, stands in the factory yard, arouses the masses and shouts: Just look at them, they only want to oppress you; throw off your chains. And upstairs his brother sees to it that those chains are well forged. On the one hand is the organ of the stock exchange, intent on encouraging ever-greater speculation. The prices of grain and all foods are driven higher and higher at an unprecedented rate. On the other hand there is the organ of the workers which arouses the masses by telling them: Bread has gone up; one thing and another has increased in price; do not tolerate it any longer; awake, proletarian . . . .

How long can this process go on? For it implies the annihilation of the economic system as well as the annihilation of a whole people. It is quite evident that this fourth estate [the workers] was not organized by the Jew just to safeguard the interests of that class. It is clear that the Jew Isaac Cohn does not stand in the factory out of love for the workers. It is self-evident that all those apostles who are talking themselves blue in the face on behalf of the workers, but at the same time patronize the Hotel Excelsior, ride in express trains, and spend their vacations in Nice, are not exerting themselves for the sake of the people. No, the people is not to derive any benefits from all this. No, the people is not to derive any benefits from all this. The people is supposed to destroy the backbone of its own independence, its own economic system so it will all the more certainly sink into the golden fetters of the everlasting interest-slavery of the Jewish race. . . .

How long can this continue? It will continue until suddenly from out of the masses someone comes forth who will seize the leadership, find more comrades, and gradually cause the anger that has long been restrained to break loose against the deceivers. This is the great lurking danger which confronts the Jew; and he has only one safeguard against it, namely, to do away with this evil national intelligentsia. This is the irrevocable and ultimate aim of the Jewish revolution. And he must pursue this aim. He knows full well that his system is no blessing, that he is no master race (*Herrenvolk*), that he is an exploiter, that the Jews are a people of robbers. The Jew has never yet founded a civilization, but he has destroyed hundreds. He can show nothing of his own creation. Everything that he has is stolen. He has foreign people, foreign workers build his temples; foreigners create and work for him; foreigners shed their blood for him. He knows no people's army" (*Volksheer*) but only paid mercenaries, who are ready to risk their lives for him. He has no art of his own, everything as either been stolen from other peoples or imitated. He does not even know how to preserve these costly possessions. In his hands they turn immediately to filth and dung. He also knows that he cannot maintain any state for any length of time. There is a difference between him and the Aryan. It is true that the Aryan has also dominated inferior peoples. But how? He went about his task, cleared the forests, transformed the wilderness into civilizations, and he did not use the inferior peoples for his own purposes but he integrated them into the state in accordance with their abilities. It was through the Aryan that art and science flourished. It was he alone who, in the final analysis, knew how to establish states.

The Jew is incapable of all this. His revolutions, therefore, must be "international." They must spread like a disease. For the Jew is incapable of building a state and saying: Look, here it is, a model for all. Imitate us! He has to see to it that the epidemic does not abate, that it is not confined to any one place, because it might otherwise consume itself there. Thus he has to spread everything internationally. And how long? Until the whole world falls in ruins and brings him down with it in the midst of the ruins. (Munich, July 28, 1922; *Voelkischer Beobachter*, Aug. 16, 1922)

Discussion Questions

1. Why do Jews, in Hitler's opinion, deserve to be reviled? Why did his anti-Semitism appeal to Germans in the 1920s?
2. Why does Hitler attack Jewish people on political grounds?

Sources

Gordon W. Prange, *Hitler's Words: Two Decades of National Socialism, 1923–1943*, Washington, D.C.: American council on Public Affairs, 1944.

Ian Kershaw, *Hitler*, London and New York: Longman, 1991.

CHAPTER 24

Harry S. Truman
The Truman Doctrine

Frantz Fanon
The Wretched of the Earth

Harry S. Truman, *The Truman Doctrine*

The thirty-third president of the United States is most often remembered for the fateful decision to use the atomic bomb that he was forced to make shortly after assuming office. However, Truman had already pursued a lengthy career in politics. He spent ten years as county judge for Jackson County, Missouri and another decade in the Senate. Born in 1884 in Lamar, Missouri, Truman spent the first decade of is adult life as a farmer. He served in World War I, and when he returned home, he became active in the Democratic party. His political career led him to the vice presidential nomination in 1944, despite the fact that he was not a well-known politician. The death of Franklin Roosevelt in the spring of 1945 hurtled Truman into the limelight.

When he assumed the office of the presidency, Truman faced the enormous tasks of concluding World War II, restoring peace and prosperity to war-torn Europe, and fighting communism when it became apparent that the Soviets had ambitions in eastern Europe. These tasks required forging a new foreign policy for the United States. In a speech preceding his announcement of the policy that came to be known as *The Truman Doctrine*, the president laid the foundations for broader American economic commitments internationally. He chastised the retreat into isolationism, and urged Americans to commit to promoting free trade and economic recovery around the globe. Peace, freedom, and trade were inextricably linked, he claimed. Americans themselves would become subject to curbs on their freedoms if economic troubles on a global scale forced governmental intervention at home.

Civil war and the threat of communist victories in Greece and Turkey prompted President Truman to address a joint session of Congress in March of 1947 to solicit U.S. assistance. Truman exhorted the American public to embrace its leadership role in preserving the freedoms with which the United States was identified. The statement, found below in its entirety, clarified the Truman administration's Cold War policy, but created opposition from critics concerned with the lack of limitations that the policy imposed on American involvement around the globe.

THE TRUMAN DOCTRINE

Harry S. Truman

The gravity of the situation which confronts the world today necessitates my appearance before a joint session of the Congress. The foreign policy and the national security of this country are involved.

One aspect of the present situation, which I wish to present to you at this time for your consideration and decision, concerns Greece and Turkey. The United States has received from the Greek government an urgent appeal for financial and economic assistance. Preliminary reports from the American Economic Mission now in Greece and reports from the American Ambassador in Greece corroborate the statement of the Greek government that assistance is imperative if Greece is to survive as a free nation. I do not believe that the American people and the Congress wish to turn a deaf ear to the appeal of the Greek government.

Greece is not a rich country. Lack of sufficient natural resources has always forced the Greek people to work hard to make both ends meet. Since 1940 this industrious and peace-loving country has suffered invasion, four years of cruel enemy occupation, and bitter internal strife.

When forces of liberation entered Greece they found that the retreating Germans had destroyed virtually all the railways, roads, port facilities, communications, and merchant marine. More than a thousand villages had been burned. Eighty-five per cent of the children were tubercular. Livestock, poultry, and draft animals had almost disappeared. Inflation had wiped out practically all savings. As a result of these tragic conditions a military minority, exploiting human want and misery, was able to create political chaos which, until now, has made economic recovery impossible.

Greece is today without funds to finance the importation of those goods which are essential to bare subsistence. Under these circumstances the people of Greece cannot make progress in solving their problems of reconstruction. Greece is in desperate need of financial and economic assistance to enable it to resume purchases of food, clothing, fuel, and seeds. These are indispensable for the subsistence of its people and are obtainable only from abroad. Greece must have help to import the goods necessary to restore internal order and security, so essential for economic and political recovery.

The Greek government has also asked for the assistance of experienced American administrators, economists, and technicians to insure that the financial and other aid given to Greece shall be used effectively in creating a stable and self-sustaining economy and in improving its public administration.

The very existence of the Greek state is today threatened by the terrorist activities of several thousand armed men, led by communists, who defy the government's authority at a number of points, particularly along the northern boundaries. A commission appointed by the United Nations Security Council is at present investigating disturbed conditions in northern Greece and alleged border violations along the frontier between Greece on the one hand and Albania, Bulgaria, and Yugoslavia on the other. Meanwhile, the Greek government is unable to cope with the situation. The Greek army is small and poorly equipped. It needs supplies and equipment if it is to restore the authority of the government throughout Greek territory.

Greece must have assistance if it is to become a self-supporting and self-respecting democracy. The United States must supply that assistance. We have already extended to Greece certain types of relief and economic aid, but these are inadequate. There is no other country to which democratic Greece can turn. No other nation is willing and able to provide the necessary support for a democratic Greek government.

The British government, which has been helping Greece, can give no further financial or economic aid after March 31. Great Britain finds itself under the necessity of reducing or liquidating its commitments in several parts of the world, including Greece.

We have considered how the United Nations might assist in this crisis. But the situation is an urgent one requiring immediate action, and the United Nations and its related organizations are not in a position to extend help of the kind that is required.

It is important to note that the Greek government has asked for our aid in utilizing effectively the financial and other assistance we may give to Greece and in improving its public administration. It is of the utmost importance that we supervise the use of any funds made available to Greece, in such a manner that each dollar spent will count toward making Greece self-supporting and will help to build an economy in which a healthy democracy can flourish.

No government is perfect. One of the chief virtues of a democracy, however, is that its defects are always visible and under democratic processes can be pointed out and corrected. The government of Greece is not perfect. Nevertheless it represents 85 per cent of the members of the Greek Parliament who were chosen in an election last year. Foreign observers, including 692 Americans, considered this election to be a fair expression of the views of the Greek people.

The Greek government has been operating in an atmosphere of chaos and extremism. It has made mistakes. The extension of aid by this country does not mean that the United States condones everything that the Greek government has done or will do. We have condemned in the past, and we condemn now, extremist measures of the Right or the Left. We have in the past advised tolerance, and we advise tolerance now.

Greece's neighbor Turkey also deserves our attention. The future of Turkey as an independent and economically sound state is clearly no less important to the freedom-loving peoples of the world than the future of Greece. The circumstances in which Turkey finds itself today are considerably different from those of Greece. Turkey has been spared the disasters that have beset Greece. And during the war the United States and Great Britain furnished Turkey with material aid.

Nevertheless, Turkey now needs our support. Since the war Turkey has sought financial assistance from Great Britain and the United States for the purpose of effecting that modernization necessary for the maintenance of its national integrity. That integrity is essential to the preservation of order in the Middle East. The British Government has informed us that, owing to its own difficulties, it can no longer extend financial or economic aid to Turkey. As in the case of Greece, if Turkey is to have the assistance it needs the United States must supply it. We are the only country able to provide that help.

I am fully aware of the broad implications involved if the United States extends assistance to Greece and Turkey, and I shall discuss these implications with you at this time.

One of the primary objectives of the foreign policy of the United States is the creation of conditions in which we and other nations will be able to work out a way of life free from coercion. This was a fundamental issue in the war with Germany and Japan. Our victory was won over countries which sought to impose their will and their way of life upon other nations.

To ensure the peaceful development of nations, free from coercion, the United States has taken a leading part in establishing the United Nations. The United Nations is designed to make possible lasting freedom and independence for all its members. We shall not realize our objectives, however, unless we are willing to help free people to maintain their free institutions and their national integrity against aggressive movements that seek to impose upon them totalitarian regimes. This is no more than a frank recognition that totalitarian regimes imposed on free peoples, by direct or indirect aggression, undermine the foundations of international peace and hence the security of the United States.

The peoples of a number of countries of the world have recently had totalitarian regimes forced upon them against their will. The government of the United States has made frequent protests against coercion and intimidation in violation of the Yalta agreement, in Poland, Rumania, and Bulgaria. I must also state that in a number of other countries there have been similar developments.

At the present moment in world history nearly every nation must choose between alternative ways of life. The choice is too often not a free one.

One way of life is based upon the will of the majority, and is distinguished by free institutions, representative government, free elections, guarantees of individual liberty, freedom of speech and religion, and freedom from political oppression.

The second way of life is based upon the will of a minority forcibly impressed upon the majority. It relies upon terror and oppression, a controlled press and radio, fixed elections, and the suppression of personal freedoms.

I believe that it must be the policy of the United States to support free peoples who are resisting attempted subjugation by armed minorities or by outside pressures. I believe that we must assist free peoples to work out their own destinies in their own way. I believe that our help should be primarily through economic and financial aid, which is essential to economic stability and orderly political processes.

The world is not static, and the status quo is not sacred. But we cannot allow changes in the status quo in violation of the Charter of the United Nations by such methods as coercion, or by such subterfuges as political infiltration. In helping free and independent nations to maintain their freedom the United States will be giving effect to the principles of the Charter of the United Nations.

It is necessary only to glance at a map to realize that the survival and integrity of the Greek nation are of grave importance in a much wider situation. If Greece should fall under the control of an armed minority, the effect upon its neighbor Turkey would be immediate and serious. Confusion and disorder might well spread throughout the entire Middle East.

Moreover, the disappearance of Greece as an independent state would have a profound effect upon those countries in Europe whose peoples are struggling against great difficulties to maintain their freedoms and their independence while they repair the damages of war. It would be an unspeakable tragedy if these countries, which have struggled so long against overwhelming odds, should lose that victory for which they sacrificed so much. Collapse of free institutions and loss of independence would be disastrous not only for them but for the world. Discouragement and possibly failure would quickly be the lot of neighboring peoples striving to maintain their freedom and independence.

Should we fail to aid Greece and Turkey in this fateful hour, the effect will be far-reaching to the West as well as to the East. We must take immediate and resolute action.

I therefore ask the Congress to provide authority for assistance to Greece and Turkey in the amount of $400,000,000 for the period ending June 30, 1948. In requesting these funds I have taken into consideration the maximum amount of relief assistance which would be furnished to Greece out of the $350,000,000 which I recently requested that the Congress authorize for the prevention of starvation and suffering in countries devastated by the war.

In addition to funds I ask the Congress to authorize the detail of American civilian and military personnel to Greece and Turkey, at the request of those countries, to assist in the tasks of reconstruction and

..rpose of supervising the use of such financial and material ..ice as may be furnished. I recommend that authority also be ..vided for the instruction and training of selected Greek and Turkish personnel.

Finally, I ask that the Congress provide authority which will permit the speediest and most effective use, in terms of needed commodities, supplies, and equipment, of such funds as may be authorized.

If further funds, or further authority, should be needed for purposes indicated in this message, I shall not hesitate to bring the situation before the Congress. On this subject the executive and legislative branches of the government must work together.

This is a serious course upon which we embark. I would not recommend it except that the alternative is much more serious.

The United States contributed $341,000,000,000 toward winning World War II. This is an investment in world freedom and world peace. The assistance that I am recommending for Greece and Turkey amounts to little more than one tenth of one per cent of this investment. It is only common sense that we should safeguard this investment and make sure that it was not in vain.

The seeds of totalitarian regimes are nurtured by misery and want. They spread and grow in the evil soil of poverty and strife. They reach their full growth when the hope of a people for a better life has died. We must keep that hope alive. The free peoples of the world look to us for support in maintaining their freedoms. If we falter in our leadership, we may endanger the peace of the world—and we shall surely endanger the welfare of our own nation.

Great responsibilities have been placed upon us by the swift movement of events. I am confident that the Congress will face these responsibilities squarely.

Discussion Questions

1. What threats, according to Truman, did Greece and Turkey face in the spring of 1947?

2. In Truman's view, why did it serve U.S. interests to intervene in Greece and Turkey?

Sources

Louis W. Koenig, ed., *The Truman Administration*, New York: New York University Press, 1956.

Robert H. Ferrell, *Harry S. Truman: A Life*, Columbia and London: University of Missouri Press, 1994.

Frantz Fanon, *The Wretched of the Earth*

The talented physician and psychologist and black revolutionary Frantz Fanon was born into a middle class family in Martinique in 1925. His parents encouraged their children to assimilate into the norms and culture of French society. However, Fanon's experiences and education forced him to reject the black bourgeois aspirations that he had been raised to embrace. Aimé Cesaire, the poet and proponent of *negritude* taught Fanon during his last year in secondary school. At the age of seventeen, Fanon volunteered to fight against the Nazi occupation of France. His wartime experiences prompted him to study psychiatry not only in order to assist the victims of war overcome their damaging experiences, but also to begin unraveling the complex issue of racism. He and other black volunteers had confronted the ugly specter of racism at every turn during their training in North Africa and on the battlefields of Europe.

Fanon first studied medicine in France after the war, and then successfully sat for his exams in psychiatry in 1953. He took a position in a psychiatric hospital in Algeria, and before long, had joined the National Liberation Front, or FLN. As the French dug in their heels, the Algerians likewise stiffened in their resolve to throw off the yoke of colonial rule. The French government expelled him from the colony in 1957. Fanon became a spokesperson for the FLN in Tunis, and survived several assassination attempts. He had already written several books on race and colonialism when he was diagnosed with leukemia in 1960. He hurriedly composed his last work, *The Wretched of the Earth*, shortly before his death in 1961.

In *The Wretched of the Earth*, Fanon investigated the destructive effects of racism on society and individuals. He explored how violence could shape the human psyche, and suggested radical methods of overcoming the legacy of colonial oppression. The book caused controversy because Fanon suggested that the best means for surmounting that legacy was to transform the relationship between the colonizer and the colonized through violence. In the following passage, Fanon details the effects of violence upon the colonized and elaborates his theory of liberation through violent means.

THE WRETCHED OF THE EARTH

Frantz Fanon

National liberation, national renaissance, the restoration of nationhood to the people, commonwealth: whatever may be the headings used or the new formulas introduced, decolonisation is always a violent phenonomen. At whatever level we study it—relationships between individuals, new names for sports clubs, the human admixture at cocktail parties, the police, on the directing boards of national or private banks—decolonisation is quite simply the replacing of a certain ((species)) of men by another ((species)) of men. Without any period of transition, there is a total, complete and absolute substitution. It is true that we could equally well stress the rise of a new nation, the setting up of a new State, its diplomatic relations, and its economic and political trends. But we have precisely chosen to speak of that kind of *tabula rosa* which characterises at the outset all decolonisation. Its unusual importance is that it constitutes, from the very first day, the minimum demands of the colonised. To tell the truth, the proof of success lies in a whole social structure being changed from the bottom up. The extraordinary importance of this change is that it is willed, called for, demanded. The need for this change exists in its crude state, impetuous and compelling, in the consciousness and in the lives of the men and women who are colonised. But the possibility of this change is equally experienced in the form of a terrifying future in the consciousness of another ((species)) of men and women: the colonisers.

Decolonisation, which sets out to change the order of the world, is, obviously, a programme of complete disorder. But it cannot come as a result of magical practices, nor of a natural shock, nor of a friendly understanding. Decolonisation, as we know, is a historical process: that is to say that it cannot be understood, it cannot become intelligible nor clear to itself except in the exact measure that we can discern the movements which give it historical form and content. Decolonisation is the meeting of two forces, opposed to each other by their very nature, which in fact owe their originality to that sort of substantification which results from and is nourished by the situation in the colonies. Their first encounter was marked by violence and their existence together—that is to say the exploitation of the native by the settler—was carried on by dint of a great array of bayonets and cannon. The settler and the native are old acquaintances. In fact, the settler is right when he speaks of knowing ((them)) well. For it is the settler who has brought the native into existence and who perpetuates his existence. The settler owes the fact of his very existence, that is to say his property, to the colonial system.

Decolonisation never takes place un-noticed, for it influences individuals and modifies them fundamentally. It transforms spectators crushed with their inessentiality into privileged actors, with the grandiose glare of history's floodlights upon them. It brings a natural rhythm into existence, introduced by new men, and with it a new language and a new humanity. Decolonisation is the veritable creation of new men. But this creation owes nothing of its legitimacy to any supernatural power; the ((thing)) which has been colonised becomes man during the same process by which it frees itself.

In decolonisation, there is therefore the need of a complete calling in question of the colonial situation. If we wish to describe it precisely, we might find it in the well-known words: ((The last shall be first and. the first last)). Decolonisation is the putting into practice of this sentence. That is why, if we try to describe it, all decolonisation is successful.

The naked truth of decolonisation evokes for us the searing bullets and bloodstained knives which emanate from it. For if the last shall be first, this will only come to pass after a murderous and decisive struggle between the two protagonists. That affirmed intention to place the last at the head of things, and to make them climb at a pace (too quickly, some say) the well-known steps which characterise an organised society, can only triumph if we use all means to turn the scale, including, of course, that of violence.

You do not turn any society, however primitive it may be, upside-down with such a programme if you are not decided from the very beginning, that is to say from the actual formulation of that programme, to overcome all the obstacles that you will come across in so doing. The native who decides to put the programme into practice, and to become its moving force, is ready for violence at all times. From birth it is clear to him that this narrow world, strewn with prohibitions, can only be called in question by absolute violence.

The colonial world is a world divided into compartments. It is probably unnecessary to recall the existence of native quarters and European quarters, of schools for natives and schools for Europeans ; in the same way we need not recall Apartheid in South Africa. Yet, if we examine closely this system of compartments; we will at least be able to reveal the lines of force it implies. This approach to the colonial world, its ordering and its geographical lay-out will allow us to mark, out the lines on which a decolonised society will be reorganised.

The colonial world is a world cut in two. The dividing line, the frontiers are shown by barracks and police stations. In the colonies it is the policeman and the soldier who are the official, instituted go-betweens, the spokesmen of the settler and his rule of oppression. In capitalist societies the educational system, whether lay or clerical, the structure of moral reflexes handed down from father to son, the exemplary honesty of workers who are given a medal after fifty years of good and loyal service, and the affection which springs from harmonious relations and good behaviour—all these esthetic expressions of respect for the established order serve to create around the exploited person an atmosphere of submission and of inhibition which lightens the task of policing considerably. In the capitalist countries a multitude of moral teachers, counsellors and ((bewilderers)) separate the exploited from those in power. In the colonial countries, on the contrary, the policeman and the soldier, by their immediate presence and their frequent and direct action maintain contact with the native and advise him by means of rifle-butts and napalm not to budge. It is obvious here that the agents of government speak the language of pure force. The intermediary does not lighten the oppression, nor seek to hide the domination; he shows them up and puts them into practice with the clear conscience of an upholder of the peace; yet he is the bringer of violence into the home and into the mind of the native.

The zone where the natives live is not complementary to the zone inhabited by the settlers. The two zones are opposed, but not in the service of a higher unity. Obedient to the rules of pure Aristotelian logic, they both follow the principle of reciprocal exclusivity. No conciliation is possible, for of the two terms, one is superfluous. The settlers' town is a strongly-built town, all made of stone and steel. It is a brightly-lit town; the streets are covered with asphalt, and the garbage-cans swallow all the leavings, unseen, unknown and hardly thought about. The settler's feet are never visible, except perhaps in the sea; but there you're never close enough to see them. His feet are protected by strong shoes although the streets of his town are clean and even, with no holes or stones. The settler's town is a well-fed town, an easy-going town; its belly is always full of good things. The settler's town is a town of white people, of foreigners.

The town belonging to the colonised people, or at least the native town, the negro village, the medina, the reservation, is a place of ill fame, peopled by men of evil repute. They are born there, it matters little where or how ; they die there, it matters not where, nor how. It is a world without spaciousness; men live there on top of each other, and their huts are built one on top of the other. The native town is a hungry town, starved of bread, of meat, of shoes, of coal, of light. The native town is a crouching village, a town on its knees, a town wallowing in the mire. It is a town of niggers and dirty arabs. The look that the native turns on the settler's town is a look of lust, a look of envy ; it expresses his dreams of possession—all manner of possession: to sit at the settler's table, to sleep in the settler's bed, with his wife if possible. The colonised man is an envious man. And this the settler knows very well when their glances meet he ascertains bitterly, always on the defensive ((They want to take our place)). It is true, for there is no native who does not dream at least once a day of setting himself up in the settler's place.

This world divided into compartments, this world cut in two is inhabited by two different species. The originality of the colonial context is that economic reality, inequality and the immense difference of ways of life never come to mask the human realities. When you examine at close quarters the colonial context, it is evident that what parcels out the world is to begin with the fact of belonging to or not belonging to a given race, a given species. In the colonies the economic sub-structure is also a superstructure. The cause is the consequence; you are rich because you are white, you are white because you are rich. This is why Marxist analysis should always be slightly stretched every time we have to do with the colonial problem.

Everything up to and including the very nature of precapitalist society, so well explained by Marx, must here be thought out again.

The serf is in essence different from the knight, but a reference to divine right is necessary to legitimise this statutory difference. In the colonies, the foreigner coming from another country imposed his rule by means of guns and machines. In defiance of his successful transplantation, in spite of his appropriation, the settler still remains a foreigner. It is neither the act of owning factories, nor estates, nor a bank balance which distinguishes the governing classes. The governing race is first and foremost those who come from elsewhere, those who are unlike the original inhabitants, ((the others)).

The violence which has ruled over the ordering of the colonial world, which has ceaselessly drummed the rhythm for the destruction of native social forms and broken up without reserve the systems of reference of the economy, the customs of dress and external life, that same violence will be claimed and taken over by the native at the moment when, deciding to embody history in his own person, he surges into the forbidden quarters. To wreck the colonial world is henceforward a mental picture of action which is very clear, very easy to understand and which may be assumed by each one of the individuals which constitute the colonised people. To break up the colonial world does not mean that after the frontiers have been abolished lines of communication will be set up between the two zones. The destruction of the colonial world is no more and no less that the abolition of one zone, its burial in the depths of the earth or its expulsion from the country.

The natives' challenge to the colonial world is not a rational confrontation of points of view. It is not a treatise on the universal, but the untidy affirmation of an original idea propounded as an absolute. The colonial world is a Manichean world. It is not enough for the settler to delimit physically, that is to say with the help of the army and the police force, the place of the native. As if to show the totalitarian character of colonial exploitation the settler paints the native as a sort of quintessence of evil (1. Native society is not simply described as a society lacking in values. It is not enough for the colonist to affirm that those values have disappeared from, or still better never existed in, the colonial world. The native is declared insensible to ethics; he represents not only the absence of values, but also the negation of values. He is, let us dare to admit, the enemy of values, and in this sense he is the absolute evil. He is the corrosive element, destroying all that comes near him; he is the deforming element, defiguring all that has to do with beauty or morality; he is the depository of maleficent powers, the unconscious and irretrievable instrument of blind forces. Monsieur Meyer could thus state seriously in the French National Assembly that the Republic must not be prostituted by allowing the Algerian people to become part of it. All values, in fact are irrevocably poisoned and diseased as soon as they are allowed in contact with the colonised race. The customs of the colonised people, their traditions, their myths—above all, their myths—are the very sign of that poverty of spirit and of their constitutional depravity. That is why we must put the DDT which destroys parasites, the bearers of disease, on the same level as the Christian religion which wages war on embryonic heresies and instincts, and on evil as yet unborn. The recession of yellow fever and the advance of evangelisation form part of the same balance-sheet. -But the triumphant *communiqués* from the missions are in fact a source of information concerning the implantation of foreign influences in the core of the colonised people. I speak of the Christian religion, and no one need be astonished. The Church in the colonies is the white people's Church, the foreigner's Church. She does not call the native to God's ways but to the ways of the white man, of the master, of the oppressor. And as we know, in this matter many are called but few chosen.

At times this Manicheism goes to its logical conclusion and dehumanises the native, or to speak plainly it turns him into an animal. In fact, the terms the settler uses when he mentions the native are zoological terms. He speaks of the yellow mans reptilian motions, of the stink of the native quarter, of breeding swarms, of foulness, of spawn, of gesticulations. When the settler seeks to describe the native fully in exact terms he constantly refers to the bestiary. The European rarely hits on a picturesque style; but the native, who knows what is in the mind of the settler, guesses at once what he is thinking of. Those hordes of vital statistics, those hysterical masses, those faces bereft of all humanity, those distended bodies which are like nothing on earth, that mob without beginning or end, those children who seem to belong to nobody, that laziness stretched out in the sun, that vegetative rhythm of life—all this forms part of the colonial vocabulary. General de Gaulle speaks of ((the yellow multitudes)) and Francois Mauriac of the black, brown and yellow masses which soon will be unleashed. The native knows all this, and laughs to himself every time he spots an allusion to the animal world in the other's words. For he knows that he is not an animal; and it is precisely at the moment he realises his humanity that he begins to sharpen the weapons with which he will secure its victory.

As soon as the native begins to pull on his moorings, and to cause anxiety to the settler, he is handed over to well-meaning souls who in cultural congresses point out to him the specificity and wealth of Western values. But every time Western values are mentioned they produce in the native a sort of stiffening or muscular lock-jaw. During the period of decolonisation the native's reason is appealed to. He is offered definite values, he is told frequently that decolonisation need not mean regression, and that he must put his trust in qualities which are I well-tried, solid and highly esteemed. But it so happens that when the native hears a speech about Western culture he pulls out his knife—or at least he makes sure it is within reach. The violence with which the supremacy of white values is affirmed and the aggressiveness which has permeated the victory of these values over the ways of life and of thought of the native mean that, in revenge, the native laughs in mockery when Western values are mentioned in front of him. In the colonial context the settler only ends his work of breaking in the native when the latter admits loudly and intelligibly the supremacy of the white man's values. In the period of decolonisation, the colonised masses mock at these very values, insult them and vomit them up.

This phenomenon is ordinarily masked because, during the period of decolonisation, certain colonised intellectuals have begun a dialogue with the bourgeoisie of the colonialist country. During this phase, the indigenous population is discerned only as an indistinct mass. The few native personalities whom the colonialist bourgeois have come to know here and there have not sufficient influence on that immediate discernment to give rise to nuances. On the other hand, during the period of liberation, the colonialist bourgeoisie looks feverishly for contacts with the *élite*, and it is with these *élite* that the familiar dialogue concerning values is carried on, The colonialist bourgeoisie, when it realises that it is impossible for it to maintain its domination over the colonial countries, decides to carry out a rear-guard action with regard to culture, values, techniques and so on. Now what we must never forget is that the immense majority of colonised peoples is oblivious of these problems. For a colonised people the most essential value, because the most concrete, is first and foremost the land the land which will bring them bread and, above all, dignity. But this dignity has nothing to do with the dignity of the human individual: for that human individual has never heard tell of it. All that the native has seen in his country is that they can freely arrest him, beat him, starve him: and no professor of ethics, no priest has ever come to be beaten in his place, nor to share their bread with him. As far as the native is concerned, morality is very concrete; it is to silence the settler's defiance, to break his flaunting violence—in a word, to put him out of the picture. The well-known principle that all men are equal will be illustrated in the colonies from the moment that the native claims that he is the equal of the settler. One step more, and he is ready to fight to be more than the settler. In fact, he has already decided to eject him and to take his place; as we see it, it is a whole material and moral universe which is breaking up. The intellectual who for his part has followed the colonialist with regard to the universal abstract will fight in order that the settler and the native may live together in peace in a new world. But the thing he does not see, precisely because he is permeated by colonialism and all its ways of thinking is that the settler, from the moment that the colonial context disappears, has no longer any interest in remaining or in co-existing. It is not by chance that, even before any negotiation (1) between the Algerian and French governments has taken place, the European minority which calls itself ((liberal)) has already made its position clear: it demands nothing more nor less than twofold citizenship. By setting themselves apart in an abstract manner, the liberals try to force;—the settler into taking a very concrete jump into the unknown. Let us admit it, the settler knows perfectly well that no phraseology can be a substitute for reality.

Thus the native discovers that his life, his breath, his beating heart are the same as those of the settler. He finds out that the settler's skin is not of any more value than a native's skin; and it must be said that this discovery shakes the world in a very necessary manner. All the new, revolutionary assurance of the native stems from it. For if, in fact, my life is worth as much as the settler's, his glance no longers shrivels me up nor freezes me, and his voice no longer turns me into stone. I am no longer on tenterhooks in his presence; in fact, I don't give a damn for him. Not only does his presence no longer trouble me, but I am already preparing such efficient ambushes for him that soon there will be no way out but that of flight.

(1) We have demonstrated the mechanism of this Manichean world in ((Peau Noire, Masques Blancs)), (Editions du Seuil).

(1) Fanon is writing in 1961. (Transl.)

Discussion Questions

1. What, in Fanon's estimation, is the function of violence in colonial society?
2. What kinds of obstacles must the native confront during the process of decolonization?

Sources

Frantz Fanon, *The Wretched of the Earth*, trans. Constance Farrington, New York: Grove Press, 1963.

Hussein Abdilahi Bulhan, *Frantz Fanon and the Psychology of Oppression*, New York and London: Plenum Press, 1985.

CHAPTER 25

Mikhail Gorbachev
"Report to the 27th Congress of the Communist Party of the Soviet Union, 25 February 1986"

Gorbachev, "Report to the 27th Congress of the Communist Party of the Soviet Union, 25 February 1986"

When Mikhail Sergeyevich Gorbachev was elected General Secretary of the Soviet Communist Party Central Committe in 1985, he was the youngest of the Soviet Union's eight leaders. Of peasant stock, he studied law and then specialized in agriculture while working as a party official in his native Stavropol. He transferred to Moscow in 1978, where his political fortunes rose quickly. He became the Central Committee Secretary for Agriculture as well as a Politbureau member within two short years. On the eve of his election, he charmed the western media during a visit to Canada and the UK. His reform platform targeted the Soviet Union's stagnating economy, the limited spectrum of cultural freedom, and the legacy of the Cold War, disarmament. Gorbachev even announced that the Soviet Union would not hinder the processes of democratization already underway in eastern Europe.

However, the Soviet economy continued to experience difficulties, and Gorbachev was criticized for moving too slowly. In 1990, he proposed a series of political reforms that reduced the power of the Communist Party. His greatest opposition came for those reluctant to see reforms of any sort or the clout of the party undermined. The hardliners organized a coup in August 1991 that only failed because Boris Yeltsin opposed the conspiracy. Gorbachev's political fortunes had reached their zenith. His career unavoidably declined in the aftermath of the coup. He resigned from his post as General Secretary shortly thereafter, and by the close of the year, had also given up his post as Soviet president. Gorbachev's drive for reform had unleashed the forces that would ultimately lead to his own political demise.

In the passages excerpted from this speech to the Communist Party in 1986, Gorbachev demonstrates his skill in negotiating the tensions between the past and the future. He constantly returns to the touchstones of Soviet doctrine, but also opens up the possibility for greater cultural expression and freedom of speech. He exhorts his comrades to foment the founding of a new society, but one that is nonetheless organized on the principles of Marxism-Leninism.

REPORT TO THE 27th CONGRESS OF THE COMMUNIST PARTY OF THE SOVIET UNION

Mikhail Gorbachev

3. TO REINFORCE IDEOLOGY'S LINK TO LIFE AND ENRICH PEOPLE'S INTELLECTUAL WORLD

Comrades,

"You cannot be an ideological leader without . . . theoretical work, just as you cannot be one without directing this work to meet the needs of the cause, and without spreading the results of this theory. . . That is what Lenin taught us.

Marxism—Leninism is the greatest revolutionary world view. It substantiated the most humane objective that humankind has ever set itself—the creation of a just social system on earth. It indicates the way to a scientific study of society's development as an integral process that is law-governed in all its huge diversity and contradictoriness, teaches to see the character and interaction of economic and political forces, to select correct orientations, forms, and methods of struggle, and to feel confident at all steep turns in history.

In all its work the CPSU proceeds from the premise that fidelity to the Marxist—Leninist doctrine lies in creatively developing it on the basis of the experience that has been accumulated. The intricate range of problems stemming from the present landmark character of the development of our society and of the world as a whole is in the focus of the Party's theoretical thinking. The many-sided tasks of acceleration and its interrelated aspects—political, economic, scientific, technological, social, cultural-intellectual, and psychological—require further in-depth and all-embracing analysis. We feel a pressing need for serious philosophical generalizations, well-founded economic and social forecasts, and profound historical researches.

We cannot escape the fact that our philosophy and economics, as indeed our social sciences as a whole, are, I would say, in a state that is some distance away from the imperatives of life. Besides, our economic planning bodies and other departments do not display the proper interest in carrying rational recommendations of social scientists into practice.

Time sets the question of the social sciences broadly tackling the concrete requirements of practice and demands that social scientists should be sensitive to the ongoing changes in life, keep new phenomena in sight, and draw conclusion that would correctly orient practice. Viability can only be claimed by those scientific schools that come from practice and return to it enriched with meaningful generalizations and constructive recommendations. Scholasticism, doctrinairism, and dogmatism have always been shackles for a genuine addition to knowledge. They lead to stagnation of thought, put a solid wall around science, keeping it away from life and inhibiting its development. Truth is acquired not by declarations and instructions, it is born in scientific discussion and debate and is verified in action. The Central Committee favours this way of developing our social sciences, a way that makes it possible to obtain significant results in theory and practice.

The atmosphere of creativity, which the Party is asserting in all areas of life, is particularly productive for the social sciences. We hope that it will be used actively by our economists and philosophers, lawyers an sociologists, historians and literary critics for a bold and innovative formulation of new problems and for their creative theoretical elaboration.

But in themselves ideas, however attractive, do not give shape automatically to a coherent and active world view if they are not coupled to the socio-political experience of the masses. **Socialist ideology draws its energy and effectiveness from the interaction of advanced ideas with the practice of building the new society.**

The Party defines the basic directions of ideological work in the new edition of the CPSU Programme. They have been discussed at Plenary Meetings of the CPSU Central Committee and at the USSR Practical-Scientific Conference held in December 1984. I shall mention only a few them.

The most essential thing on which the entire weight of Party influence must be focused is that every person should understand the urgency and landmark character of the moment we are living in. Any of our plans would hang in the air if people are left indifferent, if we fail to awaken the labour and social vigour of the masses, their energy and initiative. **The prime condition for accelerating the country's socio-economic development is to turn society towards new tasks and draw upon the creative potential of the people, of every work collective for carrying them out.**

It is an indisputable fact that intelligent and truthful words exercise a tremendous influence. But their significance is multiplied a hundred-fold if they are coupled to political, economic, and social steps. This is the only way to get rid of tiresome edification and to fill calls and slogans with the breath of real life.

Divergence of words from reality dramatically devalues ideological efforts. No matter how much lectures we deliver on tact and how much we censure callousness and bureaucracy, this evaporates if a person encounters rudeness in offices, in the street, in a shop. No matter how many talks we may have on the culture of behaviour, they will be useless if they are not reinforced by efforts to achieve a high level of culture in production, association between people and human relations. No matter how many articles we may write about social justice, order, and discipline, they will remain unproductive if they are not accompanied by vigorous actions on the part of the work collective and by consistent enforcement of the law.

People should constantly see and feel the great truth of our ideology and the principled character of our policy. Work and the distribution of benefits should be so organized and the laws and principles of socialist human relationships so scrupulously observed that every Soviet citizen should have firm faith in our ideals and values. Dwellings, food supplies, the quality of consumer goods and the level of health care—all this most directly affects the consciousness and sentiment of people. It is exactly from these positions that we should approach the entire spectrum of problems linked to the educational work of Party and government bodies, and mass organizations.

Exceedingly favourable social conditions are created for boosting the effectiveness of ideological work in the drive to speed up socioeconomic development. But nobody should count on ideological, political, labour, and moral education being thereby simplified. It must always be borne in mind that however favourable it may be the present situation has its own contradictions and difficulties. No concession in its assessments should be allowed.

It is always a complex process to develop the social consciousness. but the distinctive character of the present stage has made many pressing problems particularly sharp. First, the very magnitude of the task of acceleration determines the social atmosphere, its character and specific features. As yet not everybody has proved to be prepared to understand and accept what is taking place. Second, and this must be emphasized, the slackening of socio-economic development was the outcome of serious blunders not only in economic management but also in ideological work.

It cannot be said that there were few words in this matter or that they were wrong. But in practice purposeful educational work was often replaced by artificial campaigns leading propaganda away from life with an adverse effect on the social climate. The sharpness of the contradictions in life was often ignored and there was no realism in assessing the actual state of affairs in the economy, as well as in the social and other spheres. Vestiges of the past invariably leave an imprint. They make themselves felt, being reflected in people's consciousness, actions, and behaviour. The lifestyle cannot be changed in the twinkling of an eye, and it is still harder to overcome inertia in thinking. Energetic efforts must be made here.

Policy yields the expected results when it is found on an accurate account of the interests of classes, social groups, and individuals. While this is true from the standpoint of administering society, it is even truer where ideology and education are concerned. Society consists of concrete people, who have concrete interests, their joys and sorrows, their notions about life, about the actual and sham values.

In this context I should like to say a few words about **work with individuals as a major form of education**. It cannot be said that it receives no attention, but in the ideological sphere the customary "'gross" approach is a serious hindrance. The relevant statistics are indeed impressive. Tens and hundreds of thousands of propagandists, agitators, and lecturers on politics, the study circles and seminars, the newspapers and journals with circulations running into millions, and the audiences of millions at lectures. All this is commendable. But does not the living person disappear in this playing around with figures and this "coverage"? Do not ideological statistics blind us, on the one hand, to selfless working people meriting high recognition by society and, on the other, to exponents of anti-socialist morality? That is why maximum concreteness in education is so important.

An essential feature of ideological work today is that it is conducted in a situation marked by a sharp confrontation between socialist and bourgeois ideology. Bourgeois ideology is an ideology serving capital and the profits of monopolies, adventurism and social revenge, an ideology of a society that has no future. Its objectives are clear: to use any method to embellish capitalism, camouflage its intrinsic anti-humaneness and injustice, to impose its standards of life and culture; by every means to throw mud at socialism and misrepresent the essence of such values as democracy, freedom, equality, and social progress.

The psychological welfare unleashed by imperialism cannot be qualified otherwise than as a specific form of aggression, of information imperialism which infringes on the sovereignty, history, and culture of peoples. Moreover, it is direct political and psychological preparations for war, which, of course, have nothing in common with a real comparison of views or with a free exchange of ideas, about which they speak hypocritically in the West. There is no other way for evaluating actions, when people are taught to look upon any society uncongenial to imperialism through a gunsight.

Of course, there is no need to overestimate the influence of bourgeois propaganda. Soviet people are quite aware of the real value of the various forecasters and forecasts, they clearly see the actual aims of the subversive activities of the ruling monopoly forces. But we must not forget that psychological warfare is a struggle for the minds of people, for shaping their outlook and their social and intellectual bearings in life. We are contending with a skilful class adversary, whose political experience is diverse and centuries-old in terms of time. He has built up a mammoth mass propaganda machine equipped with sophisticated technical means and having a huge well-trained staff of haters of socialism.

The insidiousness and unscrupulousness of bourgeois propagandists must be countered with a high standard of professionalism on the part of our ideological workers, by the morality and culture of socialist society, by the openness of information, and by the incisive and creative character of our propaganda. We must be on the offensive in exposing ideological subversion and in bringing home truthful information about the actual achievements of socialism, about the socialist way of life.

We have built a world free of oppression and exploitation and a society of social unity and confidence. We, patriots of our homeland, will go on safeguarding it with all our strength, increasing its wealth, and fortifying its economic and moral might. The inner sources of Soviet patriotism are in the social system, in our humanistic ideology. True patriotism lies in an active civic stand. Socialism is a society with a high level of morality. One cannot be ideologically committed without being honest, conscientious, decent, and critical of oneself. Our education will be all the more productive, the more vigorously the ideals, principles and values of the new society are asserted. Struggle for the purity of life is the most effective way of promoting the effectiveness and social yield of ideological education and creating guarantees against the emergence of unhealthy phenomena.

To put it in a nutshell, comrades, whatever area of ideological work we take, life must be the starting point in everything. Stagnation is simply intolerable in such a vital, dynamic, and multifaceted matter as information, propaganda, artistic creativity, and amateur art activity, the work of clubs, theatres, libraries, and museums—in the entire sphere of ideological, political, labour, moral, and atheistic education.

In our day, which is dynamic and full of changes, the **role of the mass media** is growing significantly. The time that has passed since the April Central Committee Plenary Meeting has been a rigorous test for the whole of the Party's work in journalism. Editorial staffs have started vigorously tackling complex problems that are new in many respects. Newspapers, journals, and television programmes have begun to pulse with life, with all its achievements and contradictions; there is a more analytical approach, civic motivation, and sharpness in bringing problems to light and in concrete criticism of shortcomings and omissions. Many constructive recommendations have been offered on pressing economic, social, and ideological issues.

It is even more important today to make sure that the mass media are effective. The Central Committee sees them as an instrument of creation and of expression of the Party's general viewpoint, which is incompatible with departmentalism and parochialism. Everything dictated by principled considerations, by the interests of improving our work will continue to be supported by the Party. The work of the mass media becomes all the more productive, the more thoughtfulness and timeliness and the less pursuit after the casual and the sensational there are in it.

Our television and radio networks are developing rapidly acquiring an up-to-date technical level. They have definitely entered our life as all-embracing media carrying information and propagating and asserting our moral values and culture. Changes for the better have clearly appeared here: television and radio programmes have become more diversified and interesting, and there is a visible aspiration to surmount established stereotypes, to take various interests of audiences into account more fully.

But can it be said that our mass media and propaganda are using all their opportunities? For the time being, no. There still is much dullness, inertia has not been overcome, and dearness to the new has not been cured. People are dissatisfied with the inadequate promptness in the reporting of news, with the superficial coverage of the effort to introduce all that is new and advanced into practice. Justified censure is evoked by the low standard of some literary works, television programmes, and films that lack not only ideological and aesthetic clarity but also elementary taste. There has to be a radical improvement of film distribution and of book and journal publishing. The leadership of the Ministry of Culture, the State Television and Radio Committee, the State Film Committee, the State Publishing Committee of the USSR, and the news agencies have to draw practical conclusions from the innumerable critical remarks from the public. The shortcomings are common, but the responsibility is specific, and this must be constantly in the minds of ideological cadres.

The Party sees the main objective of its **cultural policy** in giving the widest scope for identifying people's abilities and making their lives intellectually rich and many-sided. In working for radical changes for the better in this area as well, it is important to build up cultural-educational work in such a way as to fully satisfy people's cultural requirements and interests.

Society's moral health and the intellectual climate in which people live are in no small measure determined by the state of **literature and art**. While reflecting the birth of the new world, our literature has been active in helping to build it, moulding the citizen of that world—the patriots of his homeland and the internationalist in the true meaning of the word. It thereby correctly chose its place, its role in the efforts of the entire people. But this is also a criterion which the people and the

Party use to assess the work of the writer and the artist, and which literature and Soviet art themselves use to approach their own tasks.

When the social need arises to form a conception of the time one lives in especially a time of change, it always brings forward people for whom this becomes an inner necessity. We are living in such a time today. Neither the Party nor the people need showy verbosity on paper, petty dirty-linen-washing, time-serving, and utilitarianism. What society expects from the writer is artistic innovation and the truth of life, which has always been the essence of real art.

But truth is not an abstract concept. It is concrete. It lies in the achievements of the people and in the contradictions of society's development, in heroism and the succession of day-to-day work, in triumphs and failures, in other words, in life itself, with all its versatility, dramatism, and grandeur. Only a literature that is ideologically motivated, artistic, and committed to the people educates people to be honest, strong in spirit, and capable of shouldering the burden of their time.

Discussion Questions

1. What responsibilities does Gorbachev outline for the party?
2. To what degree do you think Gorbachev intended to allow reform? In what areas do you sense resistance to reform?

Sources

M.S. Gorbachov, *Speeches and Writings*, Oxford: Pergamon Press, 1986.

Martin McCauley, *Gorbachev*, London and New York: Longman, 1998.

CREDITS

From Madame de Lafayette, *The Princess of Cleves,* translated by H. Ashton, The Nonesuch Press, 1943.

From Montesquieu, *The Persian Letters,* translated by George R. Healy. Copyright © 1964 by the Bobbs-Merrill Company, Inc. Reprinted by permission of Hackett Publishing Company, Inc. All rights reserved.

From Rousseau, *Political Writings,* translated and edited by Frederick Watkins. Copyright © 1953 by Thomas Nelson and Sons, Ltd.

From Frederick of Prussia, *The Refutation of Machiavelli's Prince or Anti-Machiavel,* translated by Paul Sonnino, Ohio University Press. Copyright © 1981 by Paul Sonnino. Reprinted by permission of Paul Sonnino.

Reprinted with permission of Simon & Schuster from Robespierre, edited by George Rude. Copyright © 1967 by Prentice-Hall, Inc. Copyright renewed © 1995 by George Rude.

From Karl Marx and Frederick Engels, *Manifesto of The Communist Party,* Authorized English Translation, edited and annotated by Frederick Engels. Copyright © 1948 by International Publishers Co., Inc. Reprinted by permission of International Publishers Co., Inc.

From *Garibaldi's Memoirs,* assembled by Elpis Melena, Anthony P. Campanella, ed., translated by Erica Sigerist Campanella, International Institute of Garibaldian Studies, 1981. Copyright © 1981 by Anthony P. Campanella.

From Friedrich Nietzsche, *Beyond Good and Evil*, translated by Walter Kaufmann. Copyright © 1966 by Random House, Inc. Used by permission of Random House, Inc.

From Erich Maria Remarque, *All Quiet on the Western Front.* "*Im Westen Nichts Neues.*" Copyright " 1928 by Ullstein A.G.; copyright renewed © 1956 by Erich Maria Remarque. *All Quiet on the Western Front.* Copyright " 1929, 1930 by Little, Brown and Company; copyright renewed © 1957, 1958 by Erich Maria Remarque. All rights reserved.

Anna Akhmatova, "The Wind of War" from *The Complete Poems of Anna Akhmatova,* Vol. II, translated by Judith Hemschemeyer, edited and introduced by Roberta Reeder. Copyright © 1989, 1992 by Judith Hemschemeyer. Reprinted by permission of Zephyr Press.